THE
AFFLUENT
NEGROES

7 PRINCIPLES FOR
MINORITY WEALTH CREATION

NEAL OATES JR.

The Affluent Negroes
7 Principles for Minority Wealth Creation

ISBN: 979-8-9918968-9-4

Book Design by Transcendent Publishing
Edited by Shelby Rawson

Printed in the United States of America.

"And ye shall know the truth,
and the truth shall make you free."

(John 8:32)

CONTENTS

DEDICATION

This book is dedicated to those whom I love and who love me back. It is for you, and because of you, I share my ideas. I welcome your feedback. The principles outlined here have always been valid, although they remained hidden from me for many years.

I wrote this book out of passion, purpose, and love. I am passionate about seeing those whom I love live lives of abundance. Before I was aware of its presence, I had a purpose to "Be World Renowned" in everything and to positively impact those I encountered. Most importantly, I wrote this book out of love for my negro brothers and sisters who have forgotten that love exists and that they are worthy of receiving it.

You hold in your hands my best effort to honor those who have opened doors for me, believed in me beyond reason, and trusted me to guide them toward better outcomes.

I dedicate this book to you in the hope that, by the end of it, you will be in one of the previously mentioned categories.

INTRODUCTION

Welcome, dear reader, to a transformative journey toward empowerment and financial prosperity. This book, *The Affluent Negroes: 7 Principles for Minority Wealth Creation,* is not just a collection of strategies and insights, it's a labor of love and responsibility, born out of two decades of research, personal experiences, and a deep desire to see minority communities thrive. As you hold these pages, you are holding a roadmap to a more abundant life, designed specifically with your unique challenges and opportunities in mind.

I love you. Yes, even though we may never meet, I still love you. I pray that you feel loved throughout this entire book. Why am I repeating love so much, so early? It's because I want to remind you where my heart is from the outset.

One of the most substantial acts of love is correction. You may call it criticism, critique, or tearing you down. However, to say that I love (value) you and yet refuse to offer a guiding hand is a show of hatred, not love. I assure you that what you hold is a tangible form of love. Nothing more, nothing less.

Author's Background and Journey

Allow me to share a bit of my story. I am Neal Oates Jr., a minority business owner, a husband, a father, and a friend. My journey has been marked by triumphs and trials, each contributing to the wisdom I now share with you. Growing up in a community where economic hardships were the norm, I witnessed firsthand the struggles that many minorities face. However, I also saw the resilience, ingenuity, and potential that lies within our communities.

While I was geographically close to the financial hardships experienced by those in my neighborhood, admittedly, they never knocked on our door. And if they did, my parents did such a terrific job of never allowing them to enter that I was none the wiser. It wasn't until I was old enough to converse with my parents about decision-making and life principles that I understood an encouraging and challenging truth:

There are principles that create and protect wealth.

I didn't know why or how my family differed from those around us during my childhood, but I was keenly aware that differences existed. We were not wealthy, but somehow, we seemed to be insulated from the economic attacks that threatened those we did daily life with. Our summers were full of laughter, trips to other states, and my birthday parties at our home, where *every* child was welcomed.

In fact, my childhood was somewhat unique for no other reason than each time my parents went to "look at a new car," we drove it home the same day. Little did I know that this was not typical for most of my peers or their families.

My path to financial independence was not a straight line. It was a series of steps built on the lessons learned from the last. There were times when doubt and fear seemed insurmountable, but faith, determination, and the guidance of mentors helped me navigate these obstacles.

Looking back at my formative years, I can better appreciate what was required from my parents and those like them to erect a protective financial fortress around our family, so poverty's attempts to breach it were futile. This journey—filled with successes and setbacks—inspired me to write this book.

While my travels are not yet complete, I am far enough along to offer guidance to those who are now where I once was. I want to provide you with the tools and insights I wish I had utilized when I started my journey. My parents attempted to instill these principles in my brothers and me.

Maybe they received and implemented them better and faster than I did. Maybe it was meant for me to take the scenic route to prosperity. Maybe one day, you and I will meet at a crossroads, and you will offer me much-needed guidance to continue my travels.

Purpose and Scope of the Book

The purpose of this book is twofold: to empower and to equip. I aim to empower you by reinforcing the belief that you can achieve great things. Greatness is within you to break every negative pattern in your life. Your background, your circumstances, and the color of your skin do not define your potential.

What defines you are your actions, your mindset, and your faith. This book will equip you with practical strategies to help you navigate the path to financial prosperity. Additionally, action items and resources provided at the end of each chapter offer tools and support to effectively implement these principles daily.

It's imperative to note that there are seven principles, not five. In choosing the title and the acronym, I felt it essential to highlight the significance of teamwork and an abundance mindset. It would have been easier to use the abbreviation N.E.G.R.O. Two fewer principles meant fewer words, less thinking, fewer edits, and a cheaper finished product.

But when has *easier* been better? Many of us were raised to believe in a "zero-sum" game where only one Black or brown-skinned person could stand atop a mountain in victory. This is evidenced by our familiarity with the "crabs in a barrel" analogy. I encourage you to remember the African proverb, "If you want to go fast, go alone; if you want to go far, go together."

I hope that you desire to go far.

The Socio-Economic Landscape for Minorities

Understanding the socio-economic landscape is necessary to appreciate the need for this book. Minorities, particularly African Americans, have historically faced systemic barriers that hinder economic progress. These challenges have created significant wealth gaps, from discriminatory lending practices to limited access to quality education and professional networks. It is no mistake nor coincidence that, for almost two decades, I have worked in the real estate industry, which is marred by blatant inequality and unjust rules targeted primarily at Blacks and African Americans.

According to a 2020 report by the Federal Reserve, the median wealth of white households was eight times greater than that of Black households. This disparity is not just a statistic, it represents real-world limitations on opportunities, quality of life, and prospects for many minority families. However, it's crucial to recognize that despite these barriers, there are numerous examples of minorities who have achieved significant economic success.

This book is designed to bridge that gap. This bridge will not be built by *them*, nor should we, as minorities, expect it to be. We have the blueprints, aptitude, and skills to overcome the gap.

The primary question that must be posed in love to you today is, "Do **you** have the ambition?" By focusing on seven fundamental principles found in the acronym N.E.G.R.O.E.S.—Network Strategically, Educate Yourself, Generate Wealth Through Entrepreneurship, Reinforce Resilience, Own It All, Excel Everywhere, and Serve Others—we can address the multifaceted challenges that minorities face and create pathways to wealth and prosperity.

Introduction to the Seven Principles

The seven principles outlined in this book are not abstract concepts but practical, actionable strategies you can start implementing today. They are:

1. **N**etwork Strategically: Building meaningful relationships that open doors to opportunities and resources.

2. **E**ducate Yourself: Committing to lifelong learning and skill development to stay ahead in a rapidly changing world.

3. **G**enerate Wealth Through Entrepreneurship: Embracing the entrepreneurial mindset to create and grow businesses that generate wealth.

4. **R**einforce Resilience: Developing the mental and emotional strength to overcome setbacks and persevere toward your goals.

5. **O**wn It All: Taking full responsibility for your actions, decisions, and financial future.

6. **E**xcel Everywhere: Striving for excellence in all areas of your life, setting high standards, and continuously improving.

7. **S**erve Others: Using your resources, skills, and time to uplift others and positively impact your community.

Each principle is a pillar, supporting the overall structure of a prosperous and fulfilling life. Together, they provide a comprehensive framework that addresses financial prosperity, personal growth, leadership development, and a service-oriented mindset.

The Role of Faith

As hesitant as I was to lay a biblical foundation for this work, I knew it would be deceptive and incomplete without such a solid base. Having a firm grasp on the reality that it's almost impossible to do anything without offending someone, I heed the advice of those who know me best. They simply instructed me to "Stand on what you believe in and what has yielded you the greatest results." Fortunately for me, those are the same.

While this book is deeply rooted in my faith in Jesus Christ, it's designed to be inclusive and applicable to readers of all beliefs. The principles of hard work, resilience, stewardship, and service are universal. Faith, for me, is the foundation upon which these principles stand, but you are invited to interpret and apply them within the context of your own beliefs and values.

A Commitment to Your Growth

Your commitment to reading this book is a testament to your desire for growth and improvement. In a world filled with distractions and quick fixes, dedicating time to personal development sets you apart.

This process will require effort, reflection, and action, but the rewards are worth it. By applying the principles in this book, you can unlock your full potential, break free from limiting beliefs, and create a life of abundance, purpose, and significance.

Let these pages inspire, challenge, and equip you with the necessary tools to achieve your dreams. Remember, the journey to wealth creation is about accumulating material wealth *AND* living a life of meaning, impact, and fulfillment.

I hope and pray that this work will reach people of all colors, races, and walks of life. If you are reading this and are not a minority, I commend you, but I am not surprised. You have a greater understanding

than most—an understanding I seek to instill in those who genu-
inely need it.

You understand that the message is almost always more important than
the messenger or the packaging, regardless of where the information
originates, your ability to identify and leverage opportunities are com-
mendable. You are the reason this book is necessary and possible. You
are the unintended example for *us* to follow.

CHAPTER I

SETTING THE FOUNDATION – BIBLICAL WISDOM

"One must have, first of all, a solid foundation."

—Sri Aurobindo

"They are like a man building a house, who dug down deep and laid the foundation on rock. When a flood came, the torrent struck that house but could not shake it, because it was well built. But the one who hears my words and does not put them into practice is like a man who built a house on the ground without a foundation. The moment the torrent struck that house, it collapsed and its destruction was complete." (Luke 6:48-49)

Biblical Principles and Wealth Creation

Beyond its spiritual teachings, the Bible offers profound wisdom on various aspects of life, including wealth creation. The principles found within its pages have guided countless individuals toward prosperity and fulfillment, whether they were aware of them or not.

At its core, biblical teaching emphasizes that God desires abundance and prosperity for His children, and we are all His children. This belief is not just about financial wealth but also encompasses well-being, purpose, and spiritual richness. The beauty and challenge of principles is that they work regardless of who applies them and stand firmly against those who neglect to obey them.

You do not have to look far to find evidence of the foregoing statements. There are thousands of books, training programs, videos, and podcasts that promise to offer the "secrets" to amassing financial wealth, photo-worthy vacations, and piles of cash for breakfast if you only subscribe, join, or follow. The compilations of secular works that are effective in producing results are usually centered around a biblical proverb, teaching, or commandment.

The difference between the authors of those works and me is that I make no apologies nor attempt to disguise the source of the "secrets."

Biblical Foundations of Wealth

Throughout the Bible, we encounter stories of characters who achieved remarkable success through their faith, diligence, and adherence to divine principles. Whether it's Solomon's wisdom, Abraham's faith, or Lydia's entrepreneurial spirit, these biblical figures exemplify the principles of wealth creation in action. By adhering to these principles, you are empowered to harness your God-given talents and resources to create wealth for yourself and the betterment of society.

Similarly, the Bible recounts examples of those who refused to heed wise counsel and strayed away from foundational teachings. As a result, many biblical stories center on the consequences these people endured, providing both a yin and yang for us as readers to explore.

The Bible teaches that wealth creation is a personal endeavor and a communal responsibility. As stewards of God's blessings, we are called to use our wealth and resources to uplift the marginalized, empower the oppressed, and advance the kingdom of God on earth. (I do not support socialism.)

As believers of God's Word, we must embrace the reality that we must try our best to care for ourselves *and* others. Far too many of us have abandoned this call. By aligning our actions with biblical principles, we can cultivate an environment of abundance and prosperity. Let us briefly look into some of these stories and the lessons they offer.

The Wisdom of Solomon

King Solomon, renowned for his wisdom, wealth, and influence, is a prime example of how divine wisdom can lead to prosperity. When Solomon became king, he asked God for wisdom to govern His people effectively. Pleased with this request, God granted him unparalleled wisdom, riches, and honor. (1 Kings 3:5-14) Solomon's story teaches us that seeking wisdom and understanding is the foundation of true wealth. His Proverbs and Ecclesiastes are filled with insights into the value of diligence, integrity, and the prudent management of resources.

The Faith of Abraham

Abraham, often called the father of faith, embarked on a journey of entrepreneurship and wealth creation when he obeyed God's call to leave his homeland. His faith and obedience led to great blessings and prosperity. Abraham's story underscores the importance of trust in divine guidance and the willingness to take bold steps to pursue one's purpose. (Genesis 12:1-4)

The Stewardship of Joseph

Joseph's journey from slavery to becoming Egypt's second most powerful man is a testament to the power of resilience, wisdom, and divine favor. Despite his numerous adversities, Joseph remained faithful and used his God-given talents to interpret dreams and manage resources effectively. His story highlights the importance of stewardship, resilience, and the ability to turn challenges into opportunities. (Genesis 37-50)

Connecting Biblical Wisdom to the Seven Principles

The wisdom of the Bible seamlessly intertwines with the seven principles outlined in this book. Each principle reflects a core biblical teaching that has timeless relevance. I grew up reading the Bible and strive daily to adhere to its principles and commandments.

I do not share that bit of information from a position of superiority but rather from a place of understanding. The Bible is a beautifully complex, God-inspired work that contains the answers we need to live fulfilled lives. The question is, "How can you implement principles that you cannot understand?"

This is where I begin my work of empowering and equipping *YOU!* Not through a scholarly understanding of God's Word, but by making the seven principles for minority wealth creation easy to understand and possible to implement daily. Let's start with a quick overview of the seven principles and the biblical wisdom of each.

Network Strategically

In Ecclesiastes 4:9-10, we learn about the importance of relationships: "Two are better than one, because they have a good return for their labor: If either of them falls down, one can help the other up." Networking strategically is about building strong, supportive relationships that provide mutual benefits. Biblical figures like Nehemiah and Ruth exemplify the power of strategic alliances in achieving great outcomes.

By embracing strategic networking, we honor the biblical principle of community, recognizing that our success is intricately linked to the success of those around us. Through intentional relationship-building and collaboration, we expand our sphere of influence, seize valuable opportunities, and navigate the complexities of wealth creation with wisdom and discernment.

Educate Yourself

Proverbs 4:7 emphasizes the pursuit of wisdom: "The beginning of wisdom is this: Get wisdom. Though it cost all you have, get understanding." Lifelong learning and continuous education are crucial for staying ahead and making informed decisions. Solomon's dedication to acquiring and imparting wisdom is a powerful model for us.

By committing to educating ourselves, we align ourselves with the biblical mandate to pursue wisdom and understanding. This alignment is crucial as it guides our actions and decisions. Through diligent study, reflection, and exploration, we expand our intellectual horizons, sharpen our skills, and equip ourselves for the challenges and opportunities ahead on the road to wealth creation.

Generate Wealth Through Entrepreneurship

Proverbs 31:16-18 speaks of the virtuous woman who "considers a field and buys it; out of her earnings, she plants a vineyard ... She sees that her trading is profitable." This passage illustrates entrepreneurial spirit, resourcefulness, and the creation of value. The Bible encourages us to use our talents and resources to generate wealth and contribute positively to society.

You are the child of the Most High! You are royalty who was created to create. Leveraging the skills, talents, and gifts that are uniquely yours is not only an opportunity but also a responsibility. Embrace the idea that you have more to contribute by taking ownership of your life and your ability to create wealth as an entrepreneur.

Reinforce Resilience

James 1:2-4 encourages us to embrace trials as opportunities for growth: "Consider it pure joy, my brothers and sisters, whenever you face trials of many kinds, because you know that the testing of your faith produces perseverance." This passage reminds us that trials and tribulations are an inevitable part of life but also serve as opportunities for growth and refinement. It's a reminder that our challenges have a purpose, and it's up to us to find it. Resilience is about maintaining faith and perseverance in the face of challenges, just as biblical figures like Job and Paul did.

Reinforcing resilience allows us to draw strength from the biblical promise that God is with us during our trials. Through faith, perseverance, and trust in His providence, we navigate life's challenges with courage and resilience, emerging more potent and more resilient than before.

Own It All

Ownership—recognizing responsibility, accountability, and authority—is a foundational principle in secular and biblical realms. Romans 14:12 emphasizes responsibility and accountability: "So then, each of us will give an account of ourselves to God."

Taking ownership of our actions, decisions, and financial future is not just about responsibility. It's about empowerment. It's about taking control of our destinies, embracing accountability for our actions, and exercising authority over our circumstances. In doing so, we honor God's call to be faithful stewards of the blessings He has entrusted to us.

Excel Everywhere

Excellence—the relentless pursuit of greatness in every aspect of life—is a central theme throughout Scripture. Colossians 3:23-24 calls us to pursue excellence: "Whatever you do, work at it with all your heart, as working for the Lord, not for human masters." Striving for excellence in all areas of life honors God and sets a high standard for others to follow.

Daniel and Bezalel are exemplary figures of excellence in their respective fields. Bezalel, tasked with crafting the furnishings for the Tabernacle, demonstrated unparalleled skill and craftsmanship in his work.

Daniel distinguished himself through his wisdom, integrity, and excellence while serving in the court of King Nebuchadnezzar.

By vowing to excel everywhere, we commit ourselves to a standard of excellence that honors God and inspires others. Whether in our professional pursuits, personal relationships, or spiritual endeavors, we strive for greatness, seeking to glorify God through our actions and accomplishments.

Serve Others

Service—the selfless act of meeting the needs of others—lies at the heart of the Bible. In Mark 10:45, Jesus declares, "For even the Son of Man did not come to be served, but to serve, and to give his life as a ransom for many." This verse encapsulates the essence of servanthood—a willingness to sacrifice one's interests for the sake of others.

Acts 20:35 teaches, "It is more blessed to give than to receive." Serving others with compassion and empathy enriches our lives and creates a positive impact. Jesus Christ, the ultimate example of servanthood, calls us to love our neighbors and serve with humility.

By aligning our actions with these biblical principles, we position ourselves for success on the journey toward wealth creation. Through strategic networking, lifelong learning, entrepreneurial innovation, resilience, accountability, excellence, and service, we honor God and fulfill our call to be faithful stewards of the blessings He has entrusted to us.

As we set forth, remember that you are capable of more than you can imagine. Let these pages guide you toward a life of abundance, purpose, and significance.

Affluence in Action

Did I know how impactful Sunday school, Wednesday night bible studies, revivals, Easter plays, and Baptist conventions would be while I was in elementary school and forced to attend them? Of course not. None of us, as kids, realized how important they would be in building a legacy of abundance.

Now I look back and realize that while our parents may not have had the seven principles mapped out as I now do, they intrinsically knew something that others didn't take the time to acknowledge. Something that is no longer prevalent. Something that has caused me to be mocked, hated, and viewed as a threat.

This is the same thing that now makes you not only the ship's captain but the ship itself. That something is the awareness that ...

First of all, one must have a solid foundation.

Affluent Thinking

- Which of the seven principles comes easiest for you?
- How much does your spirituality impact your decision-making?

For bonus content,
visit www.TheAffluentNegroes.com/Bonus

CHAPTER 2

NETWORK STRATEGICALLY

"Sticks in a bundle are unbreakable."

- Kenyan Proverb

"Two are better than one, because they have a good return for their labor: If either of them falls down, one can help the other up. But pity anyone who falls and has no one to help them up." (Ecclesiastes 4:9-10)

Network (verb) - The ***deliberate cultivation*** of professional and personal relationships to create opportunities and exchange valuable information for ***mutual growth and success.***

Importance of Networking

Continuing with the idea of building upon a solid foundation, it seems fitting that Networking Strategically would serve as the first principle for minority wealth creation. You likely have heard of networking and have probably participated in some form of networking. Unfortunately, the idea of networking that most people have—especially minorities—is incorrect.

We have been taught that networking is all about us: the number of business cards WE get, how many contacts WE add to our databases, or who WE take photos with. Networking strategically has very little to do with you individually. Strategic networking is based solely on ensuring that there is mutual benefit because of connecting.

Networking is an essential component of wealth creation and personal development. It involves building and maintaining relationships with individuals who provide support, opportunities, and knowledge. Effective networking is not about exploiting others for personal gain but creating mutually beneficial relationships to help all parties achieve their goals.

In the context of minority wealth creation, networking can be particularly powerful. It allows you to access resources, opportunities, and support systems that might otherwise be out of reach. By building a strong network, you can gain insights into different industries, learn from the experiences of others, and open doors to new possibilities. Possibilities you thought were out of reach or off limits to you or anyone else who looks like you, are from the same area you grew up in, or who lacks the proper "pedigree."

Psychological and Sociological Aspects of Networking

Networking is deeply rooted in human psychology and sociology. Social capital, the value derived from social networks, is a critical factor in individual and community success. Researchers have found that people with strong social networks tend to have better mental health, higher job satisfaction, and greater career success. The strengthening of weak ties—acquaintances and distant connections—can be particularly valuable for accessing new information and opportunities.

When was the last time you evaluated your network in terms of your mental health, relational well-being, and career success? We rarely think beyond our current circumstances, next month's bills, or the event on our calendar two days from now. Yet, studies prove that your network and your ability to strategically leverage it are vitally important.

Affluent Thinking

- How strong is your current network?

1	2	3	4	6	7	8	9	10

Weak   Strong

Biblical and Modern Examples of Strategic Networking

The Bible provides many examples of the power of networking and community. One such example is the story of Nehemiah. When Nehemiah learned about the destruction of Jerusalem's walls, he sought the help of King Artaxerxes, leveraging their relationship to gain the resources and permission needed to rebuild the city. Nehemiah's success was due to his ability to build and maintain strategic relationships.

In Ecclesiastes 4:9-10, we are reminded, "Two are better than one, because they have a good return for their labor: If either of them falls down, one can help the other up." This passage underscores the importance of building strong, supportive relationships—a cornerstone of strategic networking.

If you were to "fall" today, who do you have by your side to help you up? I sincerely hope that you can answer that question quickly, confidently, and with a multitude of individuals. If not, pause here for a moment to ponder the following questions:

- Am I really "walking alone" on my journey to affluence?
- When was the last time I recall having supportive relationships to aid me in my pursuits?
- WHY do I not have strong, supportive relationships in my life now?

Another biblical example is found in the story of Esther. Esther's relationship with her uncle Mordecai and her subsequent connection with King Xerxes were crucial in her ability to save her people from annihilation. Esther 4:14 highlights the importance of her position and the timing of her actions: "For if you remain silent at this time, relief and deliverance for the Jews will arise from another place, but you and your father's family will perish. And who knows but that you have come to your royal position for such a time as this?"

Esther's network played a vital role in the deliverance of her people. Could the same be true for you and *your* people?

Affluent Thinking

- Who are YOUR people (family, friends, employees) waiting for you to deliver them by fully utilizing your strategic networking abilities?
- How often do you remain silent when you should speak up?

Never   **Sometimes**   **Often**   **All of the Time**

In a modern context, consider the example of Tyler Perry. A deeply committed Christian, Tyler Perry's success story is a powerful example of how strategic networking, hard work, and faith can create tremendous impact. Starting from humble beginnings, Perry used his talents as a playwright and actor to break into the entertainment industry. His initial plays struggled to find audiences, but he persisted, building relationships within the theater community and among church groups.

Perry's breakthrough came when he began strategically connecting with influential figures in entertainment and forming partnerships with those who shared his vision. He leveraged these relationships to gain visibility and secure opportunities that led to the creation of his own film studio—the first major film studio owned by an African American. Tyler Perry Studios has not only become a successful business but also a platform to tell stories that resonate with diverse audiences.

Perry's journey exemplifies the power of networking and the importance of forming connections that align with your values. His work is driven by a desire to create uplifting content, often centered on themes of faith, family, and redemption—which has resonated deeply with audiences across the globe. His story illustrates how a strong network of allies and supporters, combined with a clear mission and faith-driven perseverance, can lead to extraordinary success.

Similarly, entrepreneurs like Daymond John of FUBU have leveraged strategic relationships to build successful businesses and open new avenues for minority communities.

Practical Steps to Build and Leverage Networks

Yes! I desire for you to build a world-renowned network—one envied by your highly connected counterparts and yielding bountiful financial and emotional returns. You must understand that building and leveraging a network begins with identifying the people you know and your current relationships. This includes family, friends, colleagues, mentors, and acquaintances. Reflect on these connections and consider how they can support your goals and how you can help theirs.

Affluent Thinking

- Who do you already know that is positioned to help you achieve your goals?
- Who are you connected with that can benefit from who & what you know?

Once you clearly understand your existing network, set specific networking goals. Determine what you want to achieve through networking—whether job opportunities, mentorship, business partnerships, or industry insights. Having clear goals will help you focus your efforts and make the most of your networking activities.

Attending events and joining organizations are vital steps in expanding your network. Participate in industry conferences, seminars, workshops, and social events. Join professional organizations, clubs, and community groups related to your interests and goals. These settings provide excellent opportunities to meet new people and expand your network.

Proverbs 27:17 says, "As iron sharpens iron, so one person sharpens another." Engaging in these environments can lead to mutually beneficial relationships that enhance personal and professional growth.

Building genuine relationships is crucial. Focus on creating authentic connections based on mutual respect and trust. Show genuine interest in others, listen actively, and offer help when you can. Networking is not about what you can get from others, but about creating meaningful connections. The story of Jonathan and David in 1 Samuel 18:1-4 exemplifies this kind of relationship. Their bond was based on mutual respect and loyalty, and it provided both of them with significant support throughout their lives.

Leveraging social media can enhance your networking efforts. Utilize platforms like LinkedIn, Twitter, and Facebook to connect with professionals in your field. Share valuable content, engage in discussions, and join online groups related to your interests. Social media can help you reach a wider audience and stay connected with your network.

Maintaining these connections requires regular follow-up. After meeting someone new, follow up with a message or email to express your appreciation and interest in staying in touch. Regularly check in with your contacts, share updates, and offer support. As Hebrews 10:24-25 reminds us, "And let us consider how we may spur one another on toward love and good deeds, not giving up meeting together, as some are in the habit of doing, but encouraging one another."

Giving back to your network is equally important. Offer your time, knowledge, and resources to help others in your network. By being generous and supportive, you create a positive reputation and encourage others to reciprocate. Galatians 6:2 encourages us to "Carry each other's burdens, and in this way, you will fulfill the law of Christ."

Finally, seek mentorship and be a mentor. Find mentors who can provide guidance and advice based on their experiences. Additionally, be willing to mentor others who can benefit from your knowledge and expertise. Mentorship relationships can be highly rewarding and mutually beneficial.

I was blessed to find terrific mentors upon entering the real estate industry in 2007. Gleaning from their decades of experience was invaluable and laid the path to opening my own brokerage, World Renowned Real Estate, a decade later. Knowing that I had wise counselors available to learn from, share ideas with, and turn to during uncertain times gave me the confidence to move forward when others around me hesitated, retreated, or quit altogether.

Networking Challenges and How to Overcome Them

Networking can present several challenges, including shyness, fear of rejection, and difficulty finding the right opportunities. Here are some strategies to overcome these challenges:

1. **Shyness and Social Anxiety**: If you struggle with shyness or social anxiety, start by practicing in low-pressure environments. Attend smaller events or join groups where you feel more comfortable. Over time, gradually increase your exposure to larger

networking opportunities. Remember, networking is a skill that improves with practice.

2. **Fear of Rejection**: Rejection is a natural part of networking. Not every connection will lead to a meaningful relationship, which is okay. Focus on the positive interactions and learn from any rejections. Approach networking with a growth mindset, viewing each experience as an opportunity to learn and improve.

3. **Finding the Right Opportunities**: Identify your goals' most relevant events and groups. Research industry conferences, professional organizations, and community groups that align with your interests. Utilize online platforms to find virtual events and webinars. Being intentional about where you invest your time will help you connect with the right people.

4. **Maintaining Consistency**: Building and maintaining a network requires ongoing effort. Set aside regular time each week for networking activities, such as attending events, reaching out to contacts, and engaging on social media. Consistency is key to building strong, lasting relationships.

Affluence in Action

A significant turning point in my life happened when I was formally introduced to the "3 x 5 association" concept. It expands upon the idea that we are like the five people we spend the most time with.

You may think of this as the "birds of a feather flock together," quote your parents likely repeated to caution you about the company you kept as a teenager. Research conducted by the University of Pennsylvania supports the adage. Dr. Emily Falk from the university reiterates that "high-quality relationships and networks provide understanding, support, and validation of your self-worth."

Instead of focusing on the idea that we are the average of the five individuals we spend the most time with, the 3 x 5 association states that we become the average of the five people we spend the most time with in three specific areas of our lives.

Those distinct areas are:

1. Professionally
2. Personally
3. Socially

I love this expanded association assessment because it has forced me to be intentional in my networking while in different environments. Jim Rohn famously quipped, "Show me your network, and I'll know your net worth." When I first heard this, I laughed.

Then, as I began assessing my network and net worth, I realized neither was a laughing matter. A stark reality hit me with the brutal force of a Mike Tyson uppercut from his "Mike Tyson's Punch-Out" game I spent far too much time playing on my Nintendo as a kid.

That reality was, "I don't like my current net worth. In fact, I hate it." This was the moment that I decided to implement the Network Strategically principle in my life. Never again would I haphazardly allow myself to be influenced by those I was unwilling to trade places with.

I now pose the same challenge to you. You are likely reading this book because you desire to create some form of wealth that you do not currently possess, whether it's monetary or otherwise. Will your current associations aid you in wealth creation or hinder you? When confronted with the possibility of trading places with members of your 3 x 5 association matrix are you excited or hesitant?

If you are overcome with joy and excitement, then congratulations. You are already farther along the path to wealth creation than when I started my journey. If your initial response to the previous scenario caused you to pause and rethink your current relational connections, I am here to commend you for being honest with yourself.

Honesty, however, is not enough to move you along the road to riches. You must do as I reluctantly did. You must act NOW and create your flock that will move you toward your goal of wealth creation.

Ideas to Action

- To implement these principles, create a networking plan outlining your goals, desired connections, and strategies for building and maintaining relationships.

- Within the next month, attend at least one networking event or join a professional organization.

- Contact three individuals in your current network to reconnect and offer support.

- Remember, networking is about creating mutually beneficial connections and contributing to the success of others and your own.

For additional guidance, consider reading books such as *Never Eat Alone* by Keith Ferrazzi and *The Networking Survival Guide* by Diane Darling. Websites like LinkedIn.com, Meetup.com, and Eventbrite.com offer numerous opportunities to connect with professionals and attend events. Organizations such as the National Urban League, NAACP, and Black Professional Network provide valuable resources and networking opportunities for minority communities.

Strategic networking is a powerful tool for creating minority wealth. Building and maintaining strong relationships allows you to access new opportunities, gain valuable insights, and create a support system to help you achieve your goals.

Remember, networking is about creating mutually beneficial connections and contributing to the success of others and your own. As you continue your journey, let the principles of strategic networking guide you toward greater success and fulfillment.

For bonus content, visit www.TheAffluentNegroes.com/Bonus

CHAPTER 3

EDUCATE YOURSELF

"The best way to make more money is to increase your skills and knowledge."

–Chris Hogan

"Wisdom is a shelter as money is a shelter, but the advantage of knowledge is this: Wisdom preserves those who have it." (Ecclesiastes 7:12)

Educate (verb) - To develop the faculties and powers of (a person) by teaching, instruction, or schooling.

The Value of Lifelong Learning

Relax. I'm not suggesting that you return to college or complete your GED (although either may be beneficial IF YOU choose to). In relation to *The Affluent Negroes*, educating yourself is farther reaching than institutional learning. Education is a lifelong journey, extending far beyond traditional classroom walls. It's an ongoing process of acquiring knowledge, developing skills, and cultivating wisdom.

For minority individuals seeking to create wealth, education is an indispensable tool. It empowers you to make informed decisions, adapt to changing circumstances, and seize opportunities that might otherwise be out of reach. Proverbs 4:7 emphasizes the importance of wisdom: "The beginning of wisdom is this: Get wisdom. Though it cost all you have, get understanding."

Learning and adapting are more critical than ever. The global economy constantly changes, driven by technological advancements, shifting market dynamics, and evolving consumer preferences. You must commit to continuous learning and self-improvement to thrive in such an environment. This means staying abreast of industry trends, acquiring new skills, and expanding your knowledge base.

Why Educating Yourself Matters

1. **Adaptability and Resilience**: Adapting is crucial in a rapidly changing world. Lifelong learning fosters adaptability by encouraging you to stay current with industry trends, technological advancements, and evolving best practices. This adaptability is vital for navigating the complexities of the modern economy and overcoming challenges.

2. **Empowerment and Self-Efficacy**: Self-education empowers you by building your confidence and self-efficacy. As you acquire new knowledge and skills, you become more capable of making informed decisions and taking control of your personal and professional life. This sense of empowerment is crucial for minority individuals facing systemic barriers and discrimination.

3. **Economic Opportunities**: Continuous learning opens new economic opportunities. By staying informed about emerging industries and acquiring relevant skills, you position yourself to capitalize on new job markets, entrepreneurial ventures, and investment opportunities. This proactive approach to learning can significantly enhance your financial stability and growth.

4. **Personal Fulfillment and Growth**: Lifelong learning contributes to personal fulfillment and growth. Engaging in the process of learning new things, exploring different perspectives, and challenging yourself intellectually can lead to a more enriched and satisfying life. This personal growth extends beyond financial success, contributing to overall well-being and happiness.

Biblical Encouragement for Knowledge and Wisdom

The Bible is replete with exhortations to seek knowledge and wisdom. In Proverbs 1:5, we're told, "Let the wise listen and add to their learning, and let the discerning get guidance." This verse underscores the value of being open to new information and seeking guidance from others.

Similarly, James 1:5 encourages us to seek wisdom from God: "If any of you lacks wisdom, you should ask God, who gives generously to all without finding fault, and it will be given to you."

One of the most profound examples of wisdom in the Bible is King Solomon. When God offered to grant him anything he desired, Solomon chose wisdom above wealth, power, or long life. In response, God granted him unparalleled wisdom, riches, AND honor. (1 Kings 3:5-14) Solomon's choice highlights the primacy of wisdom as the foundation for all other forms of success.

Another biblical figure who exemplifies the pursuit of knowledge is Daniel. Despite being taken captive in Babylon, Daniel distinguished himself through his exceptional wisdom and understanding. His commitment to learning and his unwavering faith earned him favor and high positions within the Babylonian and Persian empires. (Daniel 1:17-20) Daniel's story illustrates how dedication to education and faith can lead to remarkable achievements, even in challenging circumstances.

The Apostle Paul is another exemplary figure whose life demonstrates the importance of education and wisdom. Paul was well-educated, having studied under Gamaliel, a respected teacher of the law. (Acts 22:3) His extensive knowledge of Jewish law, coupled with his openness to learning and adapting to new contexts, enabled him to effectively spread the gospel across diverse cultures and regions. Paul's letters, filled with profound theological insights and practical advice, continue to educate and inspire millions worldwide.

Affluent Thinking

- What personal example do you have that illustrates the benefits of education, learning, and wisdom?

- How would you rate your motivation to "educate yourself?"

1	2	3	4	6	7	8	9	10

  None   High

- What is your preferred learning method (reading, hands-on experience, auditory, formal education)?

Strategies for Continuous Education and Skill Development

Start by identifying areas where you can enhance your knowledge and skills. This might include formal education, such as pursuing a degree or certification, or informal learning through books, online courses, and workshops. Consider fields that align with your interests and career goals and emerging industries that offer promising opportunities.

Embrace the vast array of resources available to you. The internet has democratized access to information, making it easier than ever to learn about any topic. Online platforms offer courses on various subjects, often at little or no cost. Additionally, libraries and community centers provide valuable resources and learning opportunities. By taking advantage of these resources, you can continually expand your knowledge base and stay updated on the latest developments in your field.

Engage with mentors and peers who can offer guidance and support. Surround yourself with knowledgeable and experienced individuals in your areas of interest. They can provide valuable insights, share their experiences, and help you navigate your educational journey. Proverbs 27:17 states, "As iron sharpens iron, so one person sharpens another." By learning from others and exchanging ideas, you can enhance your understanding and develop new perspectives.

Cultivate a habit of reading and self-study. Books, articles, and research papers are treasure troves of information that can deepen your understanding of various subjects. Dedicate time each day to reading and reflecting on what you have learned. This practice not only expands your knowledge but also stimulates critical thinking and intellectual growth. Consider creating a reading list that includes both classic works and contemporary publications relevant to your interests and goals.

Attend conferences, seminars, and workshops to stay updated on industry trends and network with professionals. These events provide learning opportunities from experts, gaining new perspectives, and connecting with like-minded individuals. They also offer a platform to share your knowledge and experiences, contributing to your professional development. For example, participating in industry-specific conferences can expose you to cutting-edge research and innovative practices, enhancing your ability to apply new insights to your own work.

Stay curious and open-minded. Pursuing knowledge requires a willingness to explore new ideas and challenge assumptions. Be open to learning from diverse sources, including those outside your field of expertise. This cross-disciplinary approach can lead to innovative thinking and new insights that enhance your overall knowledge. Albert Einstein famously said, "The important thing is not to stop questioning. Curiosity has its own reason for existing."

Leverage technology to facilitate your learning. Educational apps, podcasts, and webinars are convenient tools that allow you to learn on the go. Use these resources to make the most of your time, whether you are commuting, exercising, or taking a break. By integrating learning into your daily routine, you can continuously expand your knowledge and skills. Additionally, technology can provide interactive and engaging ways to learn, such as through virtual reality simulations or gamified learning platforms.

Seek opportunities to apply what you have learned. Practical experience is a crucial aspect of education. Engage in projects, internships, or volunteer work that allows you to put your knowledge into practice. This hands-on experience will reinforce your learning and provide valuable insights that can only be gained through real-world application. Additionally, teaching others can be a powerful way to deepen your own understanding. Consider leading workshops, mentoring, or writing articles to share your expertise.

Reflect on your learning journey. Take time to assess your progress, celebrate your achievements, and identify areas for improvement. Reflection helps consolidate your learning and provides clarity on the next steps in your educational journey. Keep a learning journal where you can document your experiences, insights, and goals. This practice not only enhances your self-awareness but also serves as a motivational tool to keep you focused and committed to continuous growth.

Affluent Thinking

- Which of the previously listed strategies will you commit to in the next ten days?
- What is your first step to implementing the strategy you selected above?

Affluence in Action

I am a nerd! I may be the biggest nerd you've possibly *never* met. A nerd is defined as "a person who is extremely enthusiastic and knowledgeable about a particular subject, especially one of specialist or niche interest." What a compliment to be called a nerd … right? Maybe I'm thrilled about that title now and even proudly wear it as a badge of peculiarity, but that was not the case as I grew up in a small town of only 1,100 people.

I am going against sage advice and will make an assumption here. Based on what I've already shared about my childhood, it's unsurprising to you that my brothers and I were considered the "unusual" ones in Florala, Alabama. We weren't weird (or we didn't think we were), but we also weren't the norm.

After school, we had to finish homework, even when the teachers didn't assign us any. My friends must have thought that I was either lying or crazy when they would come over to play at 3:30 and I told them I was studying. We all had the same classes, and they knew our teachers hadn't assigned any activities for the evening or weekend.

What they didn't understand at the time, but would become intimately familiar with, is that Patricia and Neal Sr. fully understood the value of the Educate Yourself principle. My parents refused to leave their sons' educations in the hands of the Alabama State Department of Education.

Summers of library reading programs and book reports to our mother on topics ranging from electrical currents to *Where the Wild Things Are* ensured that we clearly understood the value of education and educating ourselves. It should also come as no surprise that my older brother, Steven, was the salutatorian of his graduating class, and Curtis, my younger brother, was the valedictorian of his. As for me, I graduated (mind your business)!

Fast-forward twenty years, and the seeds my mother and father planted have blossomed into more than a single tree. I hope that those seeds are the beginning of a flourishing forest. Without their commitment to instilling the principle of educating yourself, I would have probably joined the ranks of the mediocre millions who never read a complete book after finishing high school.

Thankfully, they were more than "preaching parents" who told us about the importance of getting an education. They were my first mentors and visible examples of how minorities live meaningful lives while creating abundance that extends through generations.

Ideas to Action

1. To implement these principles, start by creating a personal development plan that outlines your educational goals, areas of interest, and strategies for continuous learning. Identify specific skills or knowledge areas you want to develop and set achievable milestones. Commit to dedicating a certain amount of time each day or week to your educational pursuits.

2. Explore online learning platforms to enroll in courses that align with your goals and interests and actively engage with the material.

3. Identify potential mentors who can provide guidance and support.

4. Commit to reading regularly.

5. Attend industry conferences, seminars, and workshops.

6. Leverage technology to enhance your learning experience.

7. Seek opportunities to apply what you have learned.

8. Reflect on your learning journey.

Additional Resources:

- Books: *Outliers* by Malcolm Gladwell, *Mindset* by Carol S. Dweck, *Atomic Habits* by James Clear
- Organizations: Toastmasters International, American Management Association, National Black MBA Association

A commitment to educating yourself requires a sacrifice that empowers you to achieve your goals and create lasting wealth. By committing to continuous learning and self-improvement, you can acquire the knowledge and skills needed to navigate the complexities of the modern world.

Remember, the pursuit of wisdom and understanding is a divine mandate that leads to prosperity and fulfillment. As you embrace the principle of educating yourself, you open the door to endless possibilities and opportunities for growth.

For bonus content, visit www.TheAffluentNegroes.com/Bonus

CHAPTER 4

GENERATE WEALTH THROUGH ENTREPRENEURSHIP

"Don't let anyone convince you that your dream, your vision to be an entrepreneur, is something that you shouldn't do. What often happens is that people who are well-meaning, who really care for us, are afraid for us and talk us out of it."

–Cathy Hughes

"She gets up while it is still night; she provides food for her family and portions for her female servants. She considers a field and buys it; out of her earnings she plants a vineyard. She sets about her work vigorously; her arms are strong for her tasks. She sees that her trading is profitable, and her lamp does not go out at night. In her hand she holds the distaff and grasps the spindle with her fingers. She opens her arms to the poor and extends her hands to the needy. When it snows, she has no fear for her household; for all of them are clothed in scarlet. She makes coverings for her bed; she is clothed in fine linen and purple. Her husband is respected at the city gate, where he takes his seat among the elders of the land. She makes linen garments and sells them, and supplies the merchants with sashes. She is clothed with strength and dignity; she can laugh at the days to come." (Proverbs 31:15-25)

Entrepreneurship (noun) - The activity of setting up a business or businesses, taking on financial risks in the hope of profit.

The Power of Entrepreneurship

Entrepreneurship has the power to change everything for minorities. It can make the borrower the lender, reposition the tail to the head, and elevate the slave to master! Entrepreneurship is not only important but vital for the Affluent Negroes dreaming of creating wealth.

Entrepreneurship is a powerful vehicle for wealth creation because it provides individuals with the opportunity to innovate, solve problems, and create value for society AND THEMSELVES. For minority communities, entrepreneurship offers a path to economic empowerment and independence. It enables us to take control of our financial destinies, build generational wealth, and contribute to the economic development of our communities.

The entrepreneurial spirit is characterized by creativity, resilience, and a willingness to take risks; all things that are deeply embedded in the souls of negroes. The best entrepreneurs identify unmet needs in the market, develop innovative solutions, and bring them to life through their businesses. This process requires vision, determination, and the ability to navigate challenges and uncertainties. As Proverbs 14:23 states, "All hard work brings a profit, but mere talk leads only to poverty."

Biblical Foundations of Entrepreneurship

The concept of entrepreneurship is deeply rooted in the biblical principle of stewardship. This principle emphasizes the responsible management of resources and talents entrusted to us by God. In Matthew 25:14-30, the Parable of the Talents illustrates the importance of using our abilities and resources wisely. The servants who invested their talents and generated returns were commended, while the servant who buried his talent was reprimanded. This parable highlights the value of initiative, risk-taking, and productivity.

Let me take this moment to encourage you with my perspective on the Parable of the Talents. For many years, I read the story as you likely have and thought it was "cool" that the first two servants *added* "talents" to the original sum their master initially provided them. As I studied the text early one morning, I gained a new and exciting viewpoint that their entrepreneurial endeavors did not yield an "added" bonus but a "multiplied" return.

I share this because I wholeheartedly want you to understand that wealth creation for you as a minority does not have to be linear. When we follow the principles outlined here, we can and should expect exponential blessings that come in multiples! I believe that had the master in the Parable of the Talents remained away for an even longer timeframe instead of *adding* two or five more "talents," the return provided to the master would have been three, four, or five *times* the original investment.

Another biblical example of entrepreneurship is the virtuous woman described in Proverbs 31:16-18. She "considers a field and buys it; out of her earnings, she plants a vineyard ... She sees that her trading is profitable." This passage illustrates her entrepreneurial spirit, resourcefulness, and business acumen. She leverages her skills and resources to create value and generate wealth for her household.

The virtuous woman of Proverbs 31 is of special significance to me and deserves an entire chapter; however, I cannot deviate from the aforementioned course to give her just due. If you are a woman reading this book, I highly encourage you to study her and her actions.

Many levels of discrimination and unfairness have been a reality for me and other minority men, but being a woman is not one of them. She has directly impacted my life through the example she set, which is an example that my wife steadfastly followed. Now, I am reaping the benefits of her entrepreneurial spirit.

Nehemiah, who led the rebuilding of Jerusalem's walls, also demonstrated entrepreneurial qualities. Faced with a monumental task, he mobilized resources, inspired teamwork, and overcame significant obstacles. His story, recounted in the Book of Nehemiah, exemplifies leadership, strategic planning, and the ability to turn vision into reality.

Entrepreneurial Opportunities and Types

Entrepreneurship is not limited to starting a traditional business. There are various forms of entrepreneurship, including social entrepreneurship, which focuses on creating social value and addressing societal challenges. Intrapreneurship involves entrepreneurial activities within an existing organization, where employees develop new products, services, or processes. Understanding these different avenues can help you identify the best path for your entrepreneurial journey.

Social Entrepreneurship

Social entrepreneurs leverage business principles to address social issues such as poverty, education, and healthcare. These ventures prioritize social impact over profit, although financial sustainability is still crucial. Examples of successful social entrepreneurs include Muhammad Yunus, founder of Grameen Bank, and Jessica Jackley, co-founder of Kiva. Social entrepreneurship can be particularly impactful in minority communities by addressing specific local challenges and improving quality of life.

This view of entrepreneurship is unlike what we typically think and may encourage you to consider leveraging your entrepreneurial skills. If you were raised to either seek security or only consider the "greater good" of the masses, then focus on social entrepreneurship to be WHO you were created to be while improving the lives of those around you.

Intrapreneurship

Intrapreneurship encourages employees to think like entrepreneurs within the framework of a larger organization. This approach can lead to significant innovations and improvements. Companies like Google and 3M have embraced intrapreneurship, allowing employees to spend a portion of their time on projects of their choosing. For minorities in corporate environments, intrapreneurship offers a way to demonstrate leadership, creativity, and value, potentially leading to career advancement and increased influence.

It must be stated that intrapreneurship requires finesse and discipline, which many individuals lack. Possessing the ability to undertake additional endeavors while exceeding your required workload has the potential to be more detrimental than beneficial—unless you have resolved to fully embrace the intrapreneur mindset and responsibilities. While the work may be difficult, the rewards and recognition will very likely be worth the effort.

The Entrepreneurial Mindset

The entrepreneurial mindset is distinct from the thinking habits of employees. While employees typically focus on performing assigned tasks and meeting specific job requirements, entrepreneurs are visionaries who seek opportunities for growth and innovation. Entrepreneurs think beyond the present, always looking to improve and expand their ventures. They are proactive, taking the initiative to solve problems and capitalize on opportunities.

The best entrepreneurs understand that good enough is never "good enough." The entrepreneurial-minded person understands that if something must be done, they might have to be the ones to do it. While they don't believe they are the only ones who *can* complete a task or overcome a hurdle, they are willing to accomplish the feat *if* no one else shows up to do it.

The best thing about the entrepreneurial mindset is that it can be learned. You can take specific actions to strengthen your resolve and become THAT person if you so desire.

Psychological Traits of Entrepreneurs

Successful entrepreneurs often exhibit specific psychological traits, such as resilience, risk tolerance, and a growth mindset. Resilience allows them to bounce back from failures and setbacks. Risk tolerance enables them to make bold decisions in the face of uncertainty. A growth mindset fosters continuous learning and adaptation. Understanding and developing these traits can enhance your entrepreneurial potential.

Resilience

Resilience is the ability to recover from difficulties and setbacks. Entrepreneurs often face numerous challenges, including financial hurdles, market competition, and operational issues. Resilience helps them navigate these obstacles and keep moving forward. Developing resilience involves maintaining a positive outlook, seeking support from mentors and peers, and learning from failures.

Resilience is such an important element in the creation of wealth that it is one of the seven principles. Without resilience, it's unlikely that you or anyone will experience long-term success as an entrepreneur, parent, spouse, or any other role you occupy.

Risk Tolerance

Entrepreneurship inherently involves taking risks. Successful entrepreneurs are comfortable with uncertainty and are willing to take calculated risks to achieve their goals. As Jim Rohn often stated, "I'll tell you how risky life is. You're not going to get out alive. That's risky." That is what I call risky!

Fortunately, you can work your way into being comfortable taking the calculated risk necessary to generate wealth through entrepreneurship. Building risk tolerance involves understanding the potential downsides, planning for contingencies, and developing a rational approach to decision-making.

As we previously covered with the second principle of "Educate Yourself," there is a wealth of information and resources available to everyone seeking to better themselves. To truly inoculate yourself from unnecessary risks, follow some of the best advice contained in 2 Timothy 2:15 and "Study to show thyself approved unto God, a workman that needeth not to be ashamed, rightly dividing the word of truth." You can also mitigate potential losses by using risk management strategies, such as diversification and insurance.

Growth Mindset

A growth mindset, as described by psychologist Carol Dweck, is the belief that abilities and intelligence can be developed through dedication and hard work. The traits of dedication and hard work are not sexy and enticing. They are, however, required. It will be impossible for you to grow without both traits. You will be tempted to slack off, procrastinate, and give up.

The shout for ease and entertainment will be louder and more frequent than the whisper for growth. Decide today which call you will respond to.

Entrepreneurs with a growth mindset view challenges as opportunities for learning and improvement. They are open to feedback, willing to experiment, and constantly seek ways to enhance their skills and knowledge. These are not characteristics that were embedded in many minorities growing up.

Feedback tends to feel like criticism at the end of a poisonous dart, and when thrown by a well-intended person (often a family member or friend), it has the opposite effect. It wounds almost to the point of death—not physical death, but the death of the entrepreneurial dream that we have in our heads and hearts. The feedback that we mistakenly identify as unjust criticism blinds us, resulting in the loss of our vision for THE vision.

Many minorities fear criticism and failure, which prevents them from experimenting. I was raised in a household where my parents encouraged my brothers and me to attempt all sorts of activities. We were told that failure is not as detrimental as not attempting to do a thing and living with the weight of regret or the ghost of fear forever haunting us.

I know this may not be your reality. You may have been taught that being a minority, especially in America, is risky enough and that removing as much uncertainty as possible was the best path to security and safety—physically, emotionally, and financially.

I encourage you to consider your current relationship with experimentation. Are you afraid of it, love it, or have you never considered experimentation as an option for you due to your upbringing? For you to generate wealth through entrepreneurship, you must attempt something new. Some of the endeavors will succeed. Others will not. The beauty will be found in the journey.

Our Identity as God's Children

As God's children, we are called to be leaders and not followers. Deuteronomy 28:13 affirms this identity: "The Lord will make you the head, not the tail. If you pay attention to the commands of the Lord your God that I give you this day and carefully follow them, you will always be at the top, never at the bottom."

This scripture reminds us that we are meant to lead, innovate, and create. God wants the best for us, and He has equipped us with the talents and abilities needed to achieve greatness. Let me restate my previous sentence as a declaration to and for you:

God wants the best for **_YOU_**, and He has equipped **_YOU_** with the talents and abilities needed to achieve greatness.

Understanding your divine heritage instills confidence and purpose. We are all stewards of the gifts and resources God has entrusted to us, and we are called to use them to glorify Him and serve others. The entrepreneurial journey is a manifestation of this stewardship.

By creating businesses that provide value, generate wealth, and contribute to the well-being of our communities, we fulfill our God-given potential. A potential that we cannot fully understand but hope to achieve. These are worthy goals that you can commit to achieving. They will be bigger than you and will demand you to be more than you thought you could be and accomplish more than you ever believed possible.

Modern Examples of Minority Entrepreneurs

Modern-day minority entrepreneurs continue to embody these principles. Daymond John, founder of FUBU, started his business with a modest investment and grew it into a global brand. His journey reflects the importance of perseverance, innovation, and strategic thinking.

John emphasizes the need for aspiring entrepreneurs to be resourceful, learn from failures, and continuously adapt to changing circumstances. Recognized as one of the most influential entrepreneurs of our time, Daymond John is more than a businessman. He is the embodiment of the third principle.

Oprah Winfrey's rise from a challenging childhood to becoming a global media mogul is another testament to the power of entrepreneurship. Through her production company, Harpo Productions, she has created a platform that amplifies diverse voices and stories.

Oprah's success underscores the significance of leveraging one's unique strengths and experiences to build a thriving business. The version of Oprah Winfrey that we see and love now is not the beginning version. She was forced to accept feedback, experiment, and constantly improve her skills and talents.

Steps to Start and Grow a Successful Business

Starting and growing a successful business requires careful planning, dedication, and a willingness to learn and adapt. Here are the expanded steps:

1. **Identify a Viable Business Idea**: Begin by identifying a business idea that aligns with your passions, skills, and market demand. Conduct thorough market research to understand the needs and preferences of your target audience. Analyze market trends, competitor strategies, and potential gaps in the market. This foundational work will help you refine your business concept and develop a strategic plan.

2. **Develop a Comprehensive Business Plan**: A well-crafted business plan serves as a roadmap, guiding you through the various stages of your entrepreneurial journey. Your business plan should include a detailed description of your business idea, market analysis, marketing and sales strategies, operational plan, and financial projections. A comprehensive business plan not only helps you stay focused but also attracts potential investors and partners.

3. **Secure Funding**: It is crucial to secure the necessary funding to launch your business. Explore various financing options, such as personal savings, loans, grants, and venture capital. Be prepared to present a compelling case to potential investors, demonstrating your business's viability and growth potential. Additionally, consider starting small and reinvesting profits to fuel growth, as Aliko Dangote advises.

4. **Build a Strong Brand**: Your brand identity should reflect your values, mission, and unique selling proposition. Invest in professional branding elements, such as a logo, website, and marketing materials. Consistent and authentic branding helps establish credibility and build customer trust. Effective branding involves understanding your target audience, crafting a compelling brand story, and consistently communicating your brand message across all channels.

5. **Focus on Delivering Value**: Develop high-quality products or services that meet the needs and preferences of your target market. Continuously seek feedback from customers and use it to improve your offerings. Providing excellent customer service and building strong relationships with your clients can lead to repeat business and positive word-of-mouth referrals. Focusing on delivering value involves understanding customer pain points, exceeding expectations, and creating memorable experiences.

6. **Utilize Digital Marketing and Social Media**: Digital marketing and social media are powerful tools for reaching and engaging your audience. Use platforms like Facebook, Instagram, Twitter, and LinkedIn to promote your business, share valuable content, and connect with potential customers. Digital marketing allows you to reach a broader audience and measure the effectiveness of your campaigns in real time. Effective digital marketing strategies include search engine optimization (SEO), content marketing, email marketing, and paid advertising.

7. **Embrace a Growth Mindset and Adaptability**: Entrepreneurship involves navigating uncertainties and overcoming challenges. Stay resilient, adapt to changing circumstances, and continuously seek opportunities for growth and improvement.

Surround yourself with mentors, advisors, and a supportive network that can provide guidance and encouragement. Embracing a growth mindset and adaptability involves being open to feedback, learning from failures, and staying flexible in your approach.

8. **Implement Effective Financial Management**: Proper financial management is essential for the sustainability and growth of your business. Develop a robust accounting system, monitor cash flow, and regularly review your financial statements. Implement cost control measures and explore opportunities to increase revenue and profitability. Effective financial management involves budgeting, forecasting, and making informed financial decisions. This is not fun but necessary.

9. **Scale Your Business Strategically**: Explore opportunities to scale and expand as your business grows. This may involve entering new markets, diversifying your product or service offerings, or forming strategic partnerships. Scaling your business strategically involves careful planning, resource allocation, and maintaining the quality of your products or services. Fight the urge to grow too big too fast. Be sure to not get caught up in the comparison game which often results in making ego-driven decisions that lead to the destruction of a once viable business.

10. **Evaluate and Adjust Your Strategies**: Regularly evaluate your business's performance and adjust your strategies as needed. This involves analyzing key performance indicators (KPIs), seeking feedback from customers and stakeholders, and staying informed about market trends and industry developments. Evaluating and adjusting your strategies ensures that your business remains competitive and responsive to market changes.

Affluence in Action

There was something special about my old man and his truck. I respect-fully say my old man because that's exactly who he was. Born in 1921, my father was sixty years old when I was born. (Yes, I remind Wife of my pedigree every so often … And YES, you do recall me saying that I have a younger brother as well.)

Having served in the US Navy, fought in World War II, and worked at Eglin Air Force Base for thirty-one years, he did something few minori-ties had the fortitude to do in south Alabama in the 1980s. My dad chose to open his own plumbing and electrical business.

By the time I was five years old, I already knew what I wanted to be—maybe not what, but definitely who! I wanted to be my dad. I couldn't wait to get home after school to jump in his brown Dodge D-series, column-shift pickup truck and head to a job site. Why would I want to be anyone but him?

He would be home in the mornings to see my brothers and me off to school and my mom off to work. He was there when we exited the school bus, waiting for his "gopher" (I'll explain) to head to the next job with him.

He wasn't like the other men I knew in the community. He didn't answer to anyone, or so I thought. There was no clock for him to punch, and he seemed to enjoy every client interaction. Most of the time, I couldn't believe he was being paid to do his work. Besides, most of the time, I did the "real work."

If you aren't from Alabama or have never been exposed to the Southern vocabulary, a "gopher" (go for) is usually a child or apprentice you send back to the truck to fetch the tools or materials needed to complete the task. It didn't take me to "go for" too many times before I realized I had better pay attention, learn the names of the tools, and remember where they were located on the truck.

He would often tie a wire or string to my belt loop to run throughout the attic or crawl space while he shined a flashlight through a hole in the floor or ceiling to guide me. All this while he sat in the air conditioning, chatting it up with homeowners who treated him more like a friend than a service provider.

The craziest part is that I LOVED EVERY MINUTE OF IT! There wasn't a day that I didn't look forward to riding around the tri-county area with my dad, "The Entrepreneur." He made his way, set his hours, and didn't work with jerks. He provided excellent service at fair prices, which kept business flowing until he decided on his terms that it was time to step away.

Many years later, I realized one of my childhood dreams had become a reality. I was my dad—an entrepreneur, a business owner, and a creator. Today, I continue to strive to follow the lessons he taught me through the principle of generating wealth through entrepreneurship. Lessons that have resulted in me accepting the responsibility to be more, do more, and have more than the person "giving" me a paycheck would require.

Affluent Thinking

- What is your current relationship with feedback (criticism) and experimentation?
- What factors contribute to your ability or inability to accept and leverage feedback productively?
- What ideas do you have that you need to experiment with in the next twenty-four hours?

Ideas to Action

1. Take time to discover what you truly enjoy doing or the things that come easily to you.

2. Ask people who know you well what they think you are skilled or talented in.

3. Research the ideas to see if there is enough demand for your business or if there is a gap in the marketplace primed for your introduction.

4. Develop a detailed business plan that outlines your goals, strategies, and financial projections.

5. Decide how you will fund your business (savings, family, loan, etc.).

6. Commit to building a strong personal brand and focus on delivering exceptional value to your customers.

7. Utilize digital marketing and social media to promote your business and engage with your audience.

8. Survey your customers and use them to improve your offerings.

9. Remain open to learning from your experiences and seek mentorship and support from experienced entrepreneurs.

Additional Resources

- Books: *The Lean Startup* by Eric Ries, *Start with Why* by Simon Sinek, *The E-Myth Revisited* by Michael E. Gerber

- Organizations: National Minority Supplier Development Council, Black Founders, Minority Business Development Agency

Entrepreneurship is a powerful tool for wealth creation and economic empowerment. By embracing the principles of entrepreneurship, you can take control of your financial future, build generational wealth, and contribute to the economic development of your community.

Remember, the journey of entrepreneurship requires vision, resilience, and a commitment to continuous learning and improvement. Draw inspiration from biblical wisdom and modern examples of minority entrepreneurs who have paved the way for success. Recognize that as one of God's children, you are meant to lead, to innovate, and to create. God wants the best for **YOU**, and by using **YOUR** talents and abilities wisely, **YOU** can achieve greatness and fulfill **YOUR** divine potential.

For bonus content visit www.TheAffluentNegroes.com/Bonus

CHAPTER 5

REINFORCE RESILIENCE

"We may encounter many defeats but we must not be defeated."

–Maya Angelou

"Let us not become weary in doing good, for at the proper time we will reap a harvest *if we do not give up.*" (Galatians 6:9)

Resilience (noun) - The capacity to recover quickly from difficulties; toughness.

The Importance of Resilience

Resilience is not just a trait, it's a lifeline in the journey of wealth creation. It's the ability to persevere and adapt in the face of adversity. It's what enables you to navigate setbacks, learn from failures, and continue moving forward despite challenges. For minority individuals, resilience is especially vital given the unique obstacles and systemic barriers that often accompany their pursuit of success.

The path to financial independence and prosperity is seldom straightforward. It involves risks, uncertainties, and inevitable failures. But remember, resilient individuals understand that setbacks are not the end but opportunities for growth and learning. You view challenges as temporary hurdles rather than insurmountable obstacles. As James 1:2-4 teaches, "Consider it pure joy, my brothers and sisters, whenever you face trials of many kinds, because you know that the testing of your faith produces perseverance. Let perseverance finish its work so that you may be mature and complete, not lacking anything."

To benefit from any trial, hurdle, or defeat, you must endure and overcome it. I firmly believe that God will not bring you *to* something that He doesn't intend to bring you *through*. If this was not the case He could not be considered a good and loving father.

Psychological Theories on Resilience

Understanding the psychological underpinnings of resilience can provide deeper insights into how to develop this essential trait. Research by psychologists Carol Dweck and Angela Duckworth has highlighted the importance of mindset and perseverance in building resilience.

Growth Mindset

Carol Dweck's research on mindset has shown that individuals with a growth mindset—those who believe that their abilities can be developed through effort and learning—are more resilient in the face of challenges. A growth mindset fosters a love for learning, embraces challenges, and views failures as opportunities for growth.

In relation to resilience, failure is not final. It's a pit stop on the path towards the goal. Accepting the reality that you are either growing or dying is pivotal to creating wealth. There is no stagnation, only increase or decrease.

Grit

Angela Duckworth's concept of grit, defined as passion and perseverance for long-term goals, is closely related to resilience. Grit involves maintaining effort and interest over the years despite failures, adversity, and plateaus in progress. Duckworth's research suggests that grit is a better predictor of success than talent or intelligence.

Let her research inspire you. You do not have to be skilled or talented to succeed, and you do not need the IQ of a genius to join the ranks of the elite few. You only need to possess grit and refuse to quit. Crossing the finish line is a guarantee for the runner who never stops moving forward in the correct direction.

Biblical Foundations of Resilience

The Bible provides numerous examples of resilience. One of the most profound stories is that of Job. Job faced unimaginable suffering and loss, yet he remained steadfast in his faith. Despite his trials, Job declared, "Though he slay me, yet will I hope in him." (Job 13:15) Job's story exemplifies unwavering faith and resilience in the face of extreme adversity. His perseverance was rewarded, as God restored his fortunes and blessed him with even greater prosperity.

Can you relate to Job? Many minorities believe they can in regard to the feelings of loss and the amount of suffering they have endured. If that is the only correlation between you and Job, I ask you to look at WHO Job really was.

While he experienced what most of us would call unfair circumstances, his resilience spoke for itself. Instead of hearing the story of Job and focusing on the pain, loss, and unfairness of the situation, what if you only highlight his resilience and the rewards that followed as a result?

Do you have what it takes to endure? When everything around you is falling apart and everyone has turned their backs (or worse, stayed and laughed), will you be able to stand on the dream and purpose that God placed in your heart?

Affluent Thinking

- Who in your life embodies "Job-like" resilience?
- What keeps them going when an average person quits?

Another example is the story of Joseph. Sold into slavery by his brothers and later imprisoned unjustly, Joseph could have succumbed to despair. Instead, he remained resilient and faithful, eventually rising to become the second most powerful man in Egypt. His resilience and ability to interpret dreams played a crucial role in saving Egypt and his family from famine. (Genesis 37-50) Joseph's journey underscores the importance of maintaining faith and resilience, even when circumstances seem dire.

The story of Joseph is a challenging one for me because I have brothers. As much as I love Steven and Curtis, I'm not totally sure that I could be the man that Joseph was. Yes, I know and believe that God works all things for the good of those who love and obey him (Romans 8:28) … BUT to be sold into slavery by his brothers due to jealousy only to later save them from starvation is, for lack of a better term, **WILD!**

You and I may not experience that type of betrayal nor have to muster up that amount of resilience, but the great news is that Joseph has already shown us that it is possible. If he can be that strong then so can we.

The Apostle Paul is also a powerful example of resilience. Despite facing persecution, imprisonment, and numerous hardships, Paul remained dedicated to his mission of spreading the gospel. In 2 Corinthians 4:8-9, Paul writes, "We are hard pressed on every side, but not crushed; perplexed, but not in despair; persecuted, but not abandoned; struck down, but not destroyed." Paul's resilience and unwavering commitment to his calling serve as an inspiration to persevere through difficulties.

Are you able to say that you are truly dedicated to the mission of creating wealth? If not, it's unlikely that you will persevere through the types of difficulties experienced by the three biblical examples previously mentioned. If, however, your determination runs deep and resilience has become your native language, success awaits.

Modern Examples of Resilience

Resilience is not only a biblical principle but also a trait demonstrated by many modern-day individuals who have overcome significant challenges to achieve success. Nelson Mandela, who spent twenty-seven years in prison for his fight against apartheid, emerged with an unbroken spirit and went on to become the first Black president of South Africa. His resilience in the face of prolonged adversity transformed a nation and inspired the world.

Again, Oprah Winfrey's journey from a traumatic childhood to becoming a global media icon is a testament to resilience. Despite facing numerous obstacles, including poverty, abuse, and discrimination, Oprah remained focused on her goals. Her resilience, coupled with her talent and determination, enabled her to build an empire that has touched millions of lives.

Another inspiring example is that of Maya Angelou. Angelou rose to become one of the most influential voices in literature and civil rights after overcoming the trauma of childhood sexual abuse and the subsequent years of muteness. Her resilience is beautifully captured in her autobiography, *I Know Why the Caged Bird Sings*, which continues to inspire readers worldwide.

Perhaps the most important modern-day example of resilience in action is *your* example. **YOU ARE STILL HERE!** While you may not have yet achieved massive success or be known by millions, your willingness to remain in the fight speaks volumes about who you are and what you are capable of.

Willingness …? You probably read that and thought, *I'm not here because I want to be. I'm not persevering out of willingness. I'm still fighting simply due to a lack of any other options.* If this is your stance, you are to be commended because in not thinking that you had any other options, you chose the correct option.

The same circumstances and situations that you have overcome took someone else out. What frustrated you and made you upset broke others and forced them into submission. The example of resilience that you are now setting is the greatest example that someone will ever see.

Never underestimate the value that your resilience adds to the lives of your audience. Remember that your refusal to surrender emboldens others to reinforce resilience that was once on the brink of extinction.

YOU ARE STILL HERE!

Building and Reinforcing Resilience

Developing resilience involves cultivating a mindset and habits that enable you to withstand and overcome adversity. Here are some practical steps to build and reinforce resilience:

Develop a Strong Sense of Purpose

Having a clear sense of purpose provides direction and motivation, especially during challenging times. Reflect on your goals and values and let them guide your actions. Understanding your "why" can help you stay focused and resilient in the face of setbacks.

A strong sense of purpose anchors you during turbulent times and keeps you moving forward. It reminds you of what you are working towards and why it's important. For those of us seeking to create wealth, we must always hold this purpose close to our hearts and in front of our eyes.

The world is not designed to aid you in creating wealth easily. When you find yourself wanting to violate the seven principles outlined in this book refocus on why you grabbed ahold of the desire for wealth in the first place.

Cultivate a Positive Mindset

A positive outlook can significantly impact your ability to cope with adversity. Focus on the positive aspects of your situation, practice gratitude, and maintain hope. Philippians 4:8 encourages us to think about whatever is true, noble, right, pure, lovely, and admirable.

Positive thinking can help you stay motivated and resilient. This does not mean ignoring difficulties but rather approaching them with an optimistic and constructive attitude. For example, instead of viewing a failure as a defeat, see it as a learning opportunity that will bring you closer to success.

Build Strong Relationships

We started out looking at the importance of networking strategically. Surround yourself with supportive and positive individuals who can offer encouragement and assistance. Strong relationships provide a support system that can help you navigate difficult times. Ecclesiastes 4:9-10 reminds us, "Two are better than one, because they have a good return for their labor: If either of them falls down, one can help the other up." By nurturing meaningful connections, you create a network of allies who can provide emotional support, advice, and resources during challenging periods.

Stay Adaptable

Flexibility and adaptability are key components of resilience. Be open to change and willing to adjust your plans as needed. Embrace new opportunities and learn from your experiences. Romans 8:28 assures us that "in all things God works for the good of those who love him, who have been called according to his purpose." Adaptability allows you to pivot and find new paths when faced with obstacles, ensuring you remain on track toward your wealth creation goals.

Practice Self-Care

You have been lied to! Your spouse, children, friends, or anyone else cannot nor should not be the most important people in your life. You MUST BE the most important person in your own life. Taking care of your physical, emotional, and mental well-being is crucial for resilience. Ensure you get enough rest, eat healthily, exercise regularly, and engage in activities that bring you joy and relaxation.

Psalm 23:3 reminds us that God restores our soul, emphasizing the importance of rest and renewal. Self-care replenishes your energy and enhances your ability to handle stress, making you more resilient in the face of adversity. Too many times, we attempt to be strong and resilient for others, but due to poor self-care we have neither the mental, emotional, or physical strength to show up and support the people we care about.

Set Relevant Goals

Break your larger goals into smaller, manageable steps. Celebrate your progress along the way and recognize your achievements. Setting relevant and attainable goals helps build confidence and maintains motivation. Proverbs 16:9 reminds us, "In their hearts humans plan their course, but the Lord establishes their steps."

By setting achievable milestones, you create a sense of accomplishment and forward momentum, which bolsters your resilience. This is called performance-based self-esteem. It results in either a positive or negative spiral. The more we like ourselves, the more we accomplish, which results in us liking ourselves even more. As you can probably guess, this positive spiral of setting and achieving goals raises our confidence and our belief that more victories lie ahead in our future.

The negative spiral begins when we fail to accomplish a goal, resulting in negative thoughts and self-talk. Immediately, we feel incapable of succeeding; therefore, we attempt smaller and fewer tasks with less energy and excitement. This negative spiral of performance-based self-esteem is very dangerous.

When you find yourself spiraling downward, get a victory under your belt, no matter how small or seemingly insignificant. Reinforce resilience by identifying as a winner!

Learn from Setbacks

View failures and setbacks as learning opportunities. Reflect on what went wrong, identify lessons learned, and apply them to future endeavors. Embrace a growth mindset, understanding that failure is a natural part of the journey to success. James 1:2-4 teaches us to find joy in trials, as they develop perseverance and maturity.

As you continue the path toward wealth creation, think back to a time when all you could think about was survival. For some of us, that means we only must think back to yesterday or this morning. Where did you make errors in judgment or abandon the wealth creation principles? Every setback provides valuable insights that can inform your strategies and decisions, leading to greater success if you decide and commit to learning from setbacks.

Develop Problem-Solving Skills

Effective problem-solving skills are essential for resilience. Approach challenges with a solution-oriented mindset, breaking down problems into manageable parts and exploring various options. Develop a systematic approach to problem-solving, which includes identifying the issue, generating potential solutions, evaluating alternatives, and implementing the best course of action.

Enhancing your problem-solving abilities equips you to handle difficulties more effectively and maintain resilience in the face of complex challenges. For years, I have coached thousands of clients on the importance of developing problem-solving skills. In my opinion, it's the second most valuable and profitable skill behind effective communication.

I believe that every minority seeking to create wealth should strive to become a P.P.S. (Professional Problem Solver). I am not advocating that you make it your life's mission to try to solve every problem that your family and friends bring to your doorstep. I am saying that after you have networked strategically, educated yourself, focused on generating wealth through entrepreneurship, and reinforced resilience in your life, you should become obsessed with solving BIG problems for BIG people. I can attest that it is one of the surest and fastest ways to create wealth and establish influence.

Affluent Thinking

- What experiences have you survived that help you solve problems?
- Up to this point in your life, have you been a Professional Problem Solver or only a Professional Problem Spotter? (There is a HUGE difference.)

Maintain a Long-Term Perspective

Resilience involves maintaining a long-term perspective and recognizing that short-term setbacks are part of a larger journey. Keep your focus on your ultimate goals and remember that temporary challenges do not define your overall trajectory. By maintaining a long-term view, you can stay motivated and resilient, knowing that persistence and dedication will eventually lead to success. A poor decision or result today does not permit you to throw your entire goals and plans out of the window.

Affluence in Action

Only minutes earlier, I was full of excitement about the opportunity to win the 4-H public speaking contest. Now, I could barely decipher the words on the paper in front of me through water-filled eyes and inkblots that resembled a Rorschach test more than the expertly crafted speech about Dr. George Washington Carver and the history of the peanut that I had originally placed on the lectern.

I had rehearsed the speech for weeks. I knew every word of the paper by memory. I made sure to commit each syllable to not only my head but also my heart. I sat in the audience as the other contestants delivered "okay" presentations and even offered cordial applause when they finished. After all, that's what winners do … right? There was no reason for me to believe that any other outcome was possible.

Besides, I had easily won the local and county competitions. My competitors and their parents congratulated me on my delivery, command of the stage, and the diligence that I had poured into my research. As a fourth grader, I had already defeated the best fifth graders in my area and was encouraged by a few remarks that, "the sixth graders are lucky you aren't in their division."

Yet, there I stood, stripped of any youthful arrogance or pride before a packed room of judges, contestants, and parents barely able to utter a word. The moment had gotten too big for me and in an instant, I skipped a word. ONE WORD. I can't remember what that word was today, but it was the equivalent to the word "dream" in Dr. Martin Luther King, Jr's "I have a _____" speech.

Do you see what I mean? At the time, forgetting that word made my entire speech crumble. My once beautifully constructed masterpiece was slowly crashing down to become only a pile of rubble. I hurriedly attempted to regain my composure and find my place, but it was too late.

I heard a few whispers in the hushed room followed by the tellingly slow "pity applause." The emcee had already made her way to the platform and was standing next to me, ready to put an end to my misery by encouraging the audience to give me a round of applause. I thought to myself, *Applause? They should boo me and yank me off the stage.*

As any young, humbled egomaniac would do, I scanned the room for my parents and made eye contact with my mom and dad. I fully expected to see faces of understanding, clapping hands, and gestures telling me to come sit next to them for consolation. This, however, was not what I saw. Both of my parents motioned to me to stay on the platform and keep going.

WHAT? Had they not seen what their favorite son (This may be creative liberty but that's unimportant in this story) just went through? Did they really expect me to stand in my embarrassment and finish a speech while tears careened down my cheeks? Could they not realize that not only would I not win the competition, but I was guaranteed to come in last place? Why did I have to continue? There were no participation ribbons or trophies being awarded. You either won or you didn't; some might even say you lose.

Or that's what I thought.

In hindsight, my parents knew something that I couldn't possibly understand at the age of nine. I did come in last place that day at Troy State University. My brothers did "remind me" of my abysmal failure for a couple of days afterward. And, most importantly, that day, in my failure, I became a student of communication.

Without that five-minute, gruesome experience and the journey it began for me, my life would not be as fulfilling as it is today, this book would not be a reality, and my impact in this world would be significantly diminished. In the decades since, I have studied, tested, failed, and succeeded in communication. When I've gotten it correct, I have enjoyed the harvests of well-sown seeds. At other times, my fields have been bare due to my inability to communicate effectively.

I never knew that the principle of reinforcing resilience would play such a major role in my life as it has. I'm grateful for that day. Without it, I would have given up somewhere along the way when things got difficult.

Ideas to Action

- Identify your purpose and set clear goals.
- Write down your FOUR most essential values and use them to guide your actions.
- Outwardly express gratitude to someone or for something twice daily for one week.
- Call, text, or email someone within twenty-four hours and thank them for being an example of resilience. This will benefit both of you.
- Begin to initiate voluntary change by listening to a music genre different than your usual selection or dining at a restaurant you have never visited.
- Identify how you recharge. Is it nature walks, going to the beach, hanging out with friends, or listening to podcasts?
- Schedule "recharge" time in your calendar to ensure you prioritize your self-care. Shoot for a minimum of one recharge activity every three to four days.
- Document your journey (highlights, bloopers, tears, and shouts of victory) by journaling.

Additional Resources

- Books: *Man's Search for Meaning* by Viktor E. Frankl, *Grit: The Power of Passion and Perseverance* by Angela Duckworth, *Resilient: How to Grow an Unshakable Core of Calm, Strength, and Happiness* by Rick Hanson
- Organizations: American Psychological Association, Mental Health America, The Resilience Institute

Resilience is a vital trait for achieving long-term success and navigating the journey of wealth creation. By developing a strong sense of purpose, cultivating a positive mindset, building strong relationships, staying adaptable, practicing self-care, setting relevant goals, and learning from setbacks, you can build and reinforce resilience.

Remember, as God's children, we are called to rise above adversity and lead with strength and perseverance. By embracing the principle of resilience, you can overcome challenges and achieve your goals, fulfilling your divine potential and creating a life of abundance and significance.

For bonus content visit www.TheAffluentNegroes.com/Bonus

CHAPTER 6

OWN IT ALL

"Accountability breeds response-ability."

–Stephen Covey

"Each one should test their own actions. Then they can take pride in themselves alone, without comparing themselves to someone else, for each one should carry their own load." (Galatians 6:4-5)

Ownership (noun) - The act, state, or right of possessing something; the legal right to the possession of a thing.

The Concept of Ownership

Ownership is a foundational principle in both the secular and biblical realms. It involves taking full responsibility for your actions, decisions, and outcomes. Owning your life and circumstances means recognizing you have the power and responsibility to shape your future. This principle is crucial for achieving financial independence and success. As God's children, we are entrusted with resources, talents, and opportunities and are called to steward them wisely.

Owning it all means acknowledging your role in your successes and failures, making deliberate choices, and taking proactive steps to reach your goals. It involves a shift from a passive to an active mindset, where you no longer see yourself as a victim of circumstances but as the architect of your destiny. Romans 14:12 reminds us, "So then, each of us will give an account of ourselves to God." This verse emphasizes individual responsibility and accountability.

Psychological and Economic Aspects of Ownership

Understanding the psychological and economic aspects of ownership can provide deeper insights into how to develop this essential trait. Concepts like "locus of control" and "self-efficacy" are closely related to the idea of ownership.

Locus of Control

Locus of control, a concept developed by psychologist Julian Rotter, refers to the degree to which individuals believe they have control over the outcomes of events in their lives. Those with an internal locus of control believe that their actions and decisions significantly impact their lives, while those with an external locus of control attribute outcomes to external factors such as luck or fate. Developing an internal locus of control fosters a sense of ownership and empowerment, encouraging proactive behavior and accountability.

In my library one of my favorite books is *Extreme Ownership: How U.S. Navy Seals Lead and Win* by Jocko Willink and Leif Babin. As someone with an internal locus of control, I love how the authors take a no-nonsense approach to people accepting ultimate accountability for their lot in life. I acknowledge that there are events that you have no control over, but as a functioning adult, you do have the final vote in how your life will play out.

Self-Efficacy

Self-efficacy, a concept introduced by psychologist Albert Bandura, refers to an individual's belief in their ability to succeed in specific situations or accomplish a task. High self-efficacy is associated with greater motivation, resilience, and perseverance.

Building self-efficacy involves setting achievable goals, celebrating small successes, and learning from failures. It's closely linked to taking ownership of one's life and circumstances. Without belief in oneself, very little is possible, and the giant task of creating wealth as a minority to live a big life is almost impossible.

If you weren't raised in a supportive environment that fostered a healthy belief system, you may find yourself at a disadvantage in this area, but as I have alluded to throughout this book, every principle and trait between these covers can be learned and honed. Decide and take action to develop high self-efficacy. This may require you to make serious decisions regarding your current friend group, entertainment selections, and even your health regimen.

Biblical Teachings on Stewardship and Responsibility

The Bible teaches us about the importance of stewardship and taking ownership of our actions. In the Parable of the Talents (Matthew 25:14-30), Jesus tells the story of a master who entrusts his servants with different amounts of money before leaving on a journey. The servants who invest and multiply their master's money are praised and rewarded, while the servant who buries his talent out of fear is reprimanded. This parable highlights the importance of using our resources and abilities wisely and taking responsibility for our stewardship.

Do you think that the servant who buried his talent "owned it all?" Do you believe that he took extreme ownership of the gift that was entrusted to him? Of course not. If he had, he would have been rewarded like the other two servants.

How do we know this? Romans 2:10-11 reads, "But glory, honour, and peace, to every man that worketh good, to the Jew first, and also to the Gentile: For there is no respect of persons with God." There are promises attached to extreme ownership and ultimate accountability. Contrarily, there are consequences for those seeking to shirk responsibility in hopes of being cared for unjustly.

To study another example of biblical ownership for us to follow let's revisit the story of Joseph. Despite being sold into slavery (by his brothers … I'm just reminding Curtis and Steven) and facing numerous hardships, Joseph took ownership of his circumstances and used his skills and wisdom to rise to a position of great authority in Egypt. As overseer of Potiphar's household, he demonstrated integrity and accountability in managing his master's affairs. Later, as a leader in Egypt, Joseph's ownership of his responsibilities led to the preservation of many lives during a time of famine. (Genesis 37-50)

David, entrusted with the kingdom of Israel, also exemplifies ownership. As king, he took responsibility for his role and led with wisdom and courage. Despite his flaws and mistakes, David's willingness to own his actions and seek God's guidance contributed to his success as a leader. His story, recorded in 1 and 2 Samuel, illustrates the importance of accountability and the impact of responsible leadership.

I urge you not to miss the multiple examples of accepting and refusing ownership in David's life. When he refused to take responsibility for his actions, pain, stress, and death followed. Once he decided to take ownership of his mistakes (adultery, lying, and murder) God was once again able to use him and move him toward his destiny.

Affluent Thinking

- What have you not yet taken full ownership and responsibility for?
- Where in your life have you taken your "talent" and buried it in the sand, hoping to be rewarded for poor stewardship?

Taking Control of Your Financial Future

Taking ownership of your financial future involves several key steps. First, it requires a thorough understanding of your current financial situation. This includes knowing your income, expenses, debts, and assets.

I often equate my journey to wealth creation to a family road trip. I know where I want to ultimately arrive. I know the vehicle that I'm going to drive. I have my driver's license and proof of insurance with me. I even have my navigation app open on my phone.

All these elements are useless if I cannot first determine where I currently am. If I turn off the location access on my phone and it can't ascertain my starting point, all my other preparation is worthless. In much the same way, by honestly assessing your finances, you can identify areas for improvement and set relevant goals for the future.

Financial Assessment

Start by conducting a detailed financial assessment. List all your sources of income, including salary, investments, and any side businesses. Then, track your expenses, categorizing them into fixed (e.g., rent, mortgage, utilities) and variable (e.g., groceries, entertainment) costs. Calculate your net worth by subtracting your liabilities (debts) from your assets (savings, investments, property).

Trust me when I say that I can identify with you here. You probably won't like conducting this analysis the first few times. The process may reveal a dire situation and make you realize that things are worse than you initially imagined. The best part about this exercise is that it brings you out of the darkness of ignorance and into the light of knowledge. Once you know it, you can improve it.

From 1985 to 1987 a series of public service announcements were produced starring characters from G.I. Joe. Each PSA ended with one of the "troubled kids" spouting, "Now I know!" The featured Joe would then follow it up with the famous catchphrase, "And knowing is half the battle!" This comprehensive view of your financial health will help you make informed decisions and set obtainable goals all while winning half the battle.

Develop a Comprehensive Financial Plan

Next, develop a comprehensive financial plan that outlines your short-term and long-term goals. This plan should include strategies for saving, investing, and managing debt. Proverbs 21:5 advises, "The plans of the diligent lead to profit as surely as haste leads to poverty." A well-thought-out financial plan provides a roadmap for achieving financial stability and growth.

This portion of the process will probably require some outside guidance. If you have followed the first principle of the book then you understand the value of networking strategically and may already have a reputable, skilled person in mind to assist you. If not, ask someone who appears to be financially secure about their process or for a referral to a professional who can guide you.

Budgeting

Budgeting is a crucial component of financial ownership. Create a budget that aligns with your goals and priorities and track your spending to ensure you stay on course. Living within your means and avoiding unnecessary debt are essential for building a solid financial foundation. By taking control of your spending, you can free up resources for savings and investments. Budgeting doesn't have to be intimidating or time-consuming. There are dozens of apps and programs available that can link with your bank accounts to streamline the process.

When my wife and I were first introduced to the concept of budgeting, all we could think of were the restrictions and limitations a budget would place on our lives. We possessed a misunderstanding of the goal and effectiveness a working budget would have. Begrudgingly, we started the budgeting exercise after seeking wise counsel and witnessing examples of how we wanted to live.

We were both pleasantly thrilled when, after a few months of disciplined (non)spending and investing, we noticed progress. In full transparency, we weren't rich, we just weren't quite as in debt as we previously were. That was THE small victory we needed to adopt the process of budgeting full-time. Contrary to what we believed, budgeting was not restrictive, it was liberating. I invite you into the land of freedom. Give budgeting a try. It can change your life as it has ours.

Saving and Emergency Funds

Prioritize saving by setting aside a portion of your income each month. Aim to build an emergency fund that can cover at least three to six months' worth of living expenses. An emergency fund provides a financial cushion in case of unexpected expenses or job loss, reducing stress and increasing financial security. Multiple methods of accomplishing this can be found online or in books by financial experts. The how is not as important as the when, and the when is now!

Investing

Investing is another important aspect of owning your financial future. Educate yourself about different investment options and develop a diversified portfolio that aligns with your risk tolerance and goals. Investing in stocks, bonds, real estate, and other assets can help you build wealth over time. Ecclesiastes 11:2 advises, "Invest in seven ventures, yes, in eight; you do not know what disaster may come upon the land." Diversification helps mitigate risk and increases the potential for financial growth.

While the Bible encourages diversification, it also speaks to the importance of wisdom in decision-making. The Oracle of Omaha,

Warren Buffet, is known for advising people to only invest in what they know. Do your homework before investing and research any financial investors before handing over your well-earned resources to them. Be leery of get-rich-quick schemes or opportunities that appear too good to be true.

Debt Management

Managing debt is critical for financial health but is an area where millions of people struggle annually, especially minorities who have not received adequate education about managing debt. Prioritize paying off high-interest debts, such as credit card balances, while making regular payments on other loans.

Consider strategies like the debt snowball or debt avalanche methods to systematically reduce your debt. Avoid taking on new debt unless it is for investments that will generate future income. Be sure to visit TheAffluentNegroes.com/Bonus for reputable resources to help you effectively manage debt.

Mindset Shifts for Ownership

Shifting to an ownership mindset involves several key changes in perspective and behavior. One of the most significant shifts is from a victim mentality to a victor mentality. Instead of blaming external factors for your circumstances, take responsibility for your actions and decisions. Recognize that you have the power to change your situation and make choices that lead to positive outcomes.

Victim vs. Victor Mentality

A victim mentality focuses on obstacles and limitations, often leading to feelings of helplessness and inaction. In contrast, a victor mentality emphasizes agency, resilience, and the ability to overcome challenges. Cultivating a victor mentality involves recognizing your strengths, setting goals, and taking proactive steps toward achieving them.

Being a victim is easy. It will not require anything extra of you as an individual, employee, spouse, or parent. Playing the role of victim is a conscious choice. One that allows you to point the finger at "them" or "the_____ man" (insert *white* if you really want to play the victim) and blame them for your lack of wealth, freedom, and happiness.

I have friends who have been victimized by evil men who still refuse to accept the victim title. They are the most victorious of us all. They are those who force me to gaze in the mirror and see entitlement, coward-ice, and shame. Yet, they are the ones encouraging me to play the victor and stand alongside them on the podium as the mediocre masses gawk and whisper in amazement, knowing full well that we chose the difficult but worthy road.

Short-Term vs. Long-Term Planning

Another important mindset shift is from short-term thinking to long-term planning. Owning your financial future requires a focus on long-term goals and strategies rather than immediate gratification. This means prioritizing savings and investments over discretionary spending and making decisions that support your long-term financial health.

You will be forced to decide what you want out of life and the impact you desire to have. You won't necessarily have to forgo your Starbucks latte or cancel your Netflix account, but then again, you may. That's something that only you can decide. What we all must decide is whether we will follow the advice attributed to the genius Anonymous, "Plan as if you will live forever. Live as if you will die today."

Practical Steps to Take Ownership

Taking practical steps to own your financial future involves:

1. **Conducting a Financial Assessment**: Begin by evaluating your current financial situation. List your income, expenses, debts,

and assets to get a clear picture of your financial health. This assessment will help you identify areas for improvement and set realistic goals.

2. **Setting Clear Financial Goals**: Define your short-term and long-term financial goals. Short-term goals might include paying off debt or building an emergency fund, while long-term goals could involve saving for retirement or purchasing a home. Having clear goals provides direction and motivation.

3. **Creating a Budget**: Develop a budget that aligns with your goals and priorities. Track your spending and adjust as needed to stay on course. Ensure that your budget includes allocations for savings and investments.

4. **Developing a Financial Plan**: Create a comprehensive financial plan that outlines strategies for saving, investing, and managing debt. This plan should be tailored to your goals and risk tolerance. Regularly review and update your plan to reflect changes in your circumstances and objectives.

5. **Educating Yourself**: Invest time in learning about personal finance and investment options. Read books, attend seminars, and seek advice from financial experts. Knowledge is a powerful tool for making informed decisions and taking control of your financial future.

6. **Investing Wisely**: Build a diversified investment portfolio that aligns with your goals and risk tolerance. Consider a mix of stocks, bonds, real estate, and other assets to mitigate risk and maximize returns. Review your investments regularly and adjust as needed.

7. **Monitoring Your Progress**: Review your financial situation regularly and track your progress toward your goals. Celebrate your achievements and adjust as needed to stay on course. Monitoring your progress helps you stay accountable and motivated.

8. **Seeking Professional Advice**: If needed, seek the advice of financial professionals, such as advisors or planners, to help you develop and implement your financial plan. Professional guidance can provide valuable insights and help you navigate complex financial decisions.

Overcoming Common Obstacles to Ownership

Taking ownership of your financial future can be challenging, especially when faced with common obstacles. Here are some strategies to overcome these challenges:

1. **Fear of Failure**: Fear of failure can prevent you from taking risks and pursuing opportunities. To overcome this fear, reframe failure as a learning experience and a natural part of the journey to success. Remember that every setback provides valuable lessons that can help you improve and grow.

2. **Lack of Knowledge**: A lack of financial knowledge can hinder your ability to make informed decisions. Invest time in educating yourself about personal finance and investment options. Seek out resources, attend seminars, and engage with financial experts to build your knowledge and confidence.

3. **Procrastination**: Procrastination can delay progress and prevent you from acting. Combat procrastination by setting clear goals, creating a plan of action, and breaking tasks into manageable steps. Hold yourself accountable and stay committed to your goals.

4. **Limiting Beliefs**: Limiting beliefs about money and success can sabotage your efforts. Challenge these beliefs by examining their origins and replacing them with empowering thoughts. Surround yourself with positive influences and seek out success stories that inspire and motivate you.

5. **External Pressures**: External pressures, such as societal expectations and peer influence, can distract you from your goals. Stay focused on your vision and values and make decisions that align with your long-term objectives. Establish boundaries and prioritize your financial well-being.

Affluence in Action

You can tell how much a person believes in something based on their actions more than their words. How much do I believe in the principle of Own It All? My belief is so deep that ownership has been my specialty since 2006—when I entered the real estate industry. As cliché as it sounds, I didn't get into the industry because of the money but to help individuals and families realize their home ownership goals.

In my career, I've worked with renters, sellers, and investors, but there's something special about helping a buyer transition into ownership. It signifies a new level of responsibility and maturity—a willingness to rise above the minimal roles of user or consumer to owner.

The Own it All principle is also why I launched World Renowned Coaching & Consulting. After seeing how minority owners of service-based businesses struggled to find their places in the economic landscape, I realized that ownership alone wasn't enough. That's why World Renowned Coaching & Consulting has a simple mission communicated via our slogan, "Turning Owners Into Leaders."

If you don't yet own your own home or are interested in "Owning It All" through real estate investing, I encourage you to visit www.WorldRenownedRealEstate.com to schedule an initial consultation with me or one of my team members.

For business owners interested in increasing revenue, reducing effort, and attracting new opportunities, schedule a discovery consultation at www.WorldRenownedCoaching.com.

Ideas to Action

- Get a full credit report to assess your current credit situation. You can obtain one from numerous sources online, your bank, or by visiting www.AnnualCreditReport.com
- Download a budgeting app and input your fixed and variable monthly costs.
- Consult with a professional financial advisor to discuss your goals, options, and your path to success.

Additional Resources

- Books: *Rich Dad Poor Dad* by Robert T. Kiyosaki, *The Total Money Makeover* by Dave Ramsey, *Your Money or Your Life* by Vicki Robin
- Organizations: Financial Planning Association, National Association of Personal Financial Advisors, BetterInvesting.org

Ownership is a vital principle for achieving financial independence and success. By taking responsibility for your actions, decisions, and outcomes, you can shape your future and achieve your goals. Remember, as God's children, we are called to be stewards of the resources and talents entrusted to us.

By embracing the principle of ownership, you can take control of your financial future, build generational wealth, and fulfill your divine potential. Recognize that ownership is not just about possessing material wealth, but also about taking charge of your life, making deliberate choices, and striving for excellence in all that you do.

For bonus content visit www.TheAffluentNegroes.com/Bonus

CHAPTER 7

EXCEL EVERYWHERE

"Excellence is not a skill. It is an attitude."

–Ralph Marston

"Then Daniel was preferred above the presidents and princes because an excellent spirit was in him; and the king thought to set him over the whole realm." (Daniel 6:3)

Excellence (noun) - The quality of being outstanding or extremely good.

The Pursuit of Excellence

Excellence is a pursuit, not a destination. It's the continuous striving to perform at the highest level in all areas of life. Whether in your personal life, professional career, or community involvement, the commitment to excellence sets you apart and drives you toward success. As minority individuals seeking to create wealth and make a positive impact, the pursuit of excellence is crucial. It involves setting high standards, continuously improving, and consistently delivering outstanding results.

The Bible encourages us to pursue excellence in all we do. Colossians 3:23-24 instructs, "Whatever you do, work at it with all your heart, as working for the Lord, not for human masters, since you know that you will receive an inheritance from the Lord as a reward. It is the Lord Christ you are serving." This passage underscores the importance of dedicating ourselves fully to our tasks and striving for the highest standards of performance.

Excellence is not about perfection, but about giving your best effort and continually improving. It requires a commitment to high standards, attention to detail, and a proactive approach to personal and professional development. Excellence is a habit, formed through consistent effort and a dedication to growth.

Affluent Thinking

- Do you consistently "Excel Everywhere?"
- If so, where did your drive to excel originate?
- If not, why not?

Excellence in Your Personal Life

Excellence in your personal life involves nurturing your physical, emotional, and spiritual well-being. It requires setting high standards for self-care, personal growth, and relationships. By committing to personal excellence, you create a strong foundation that supports your professional and community endeavors. I have yet to meet a truly successful individual who did not exhibit excellence in their personal life. In your pursuit of wealth, don't forget that having stockpiles of money isn't the same as being wealthy.

Physical Well-Being

Taking care of your physical health is essential for achieving excellence. This involves maintaining a balanced diet, engaging in regular exercise, and getting adequate rest. Your physical health impacts your energy levels, productivity, and overall well-being. Prioritizing self-care and healthy habits ensures that you have the stamina and vitality to excel in all areas of your life. None of us desire to be the wealthiest person in the graveyard. (I'm making that assumption for you).

Emotional Well-Being

Emotional well-being is equally important. Develop healthy coping mechanisms for managing stress and seek support when needed. Practicing mindfulness, meditation, and other stress-reduction techniques can enhance your emotional resilience and help you maintain a positive outlook. Building strong relationships and fostering a supportive network also contributes to emotional well-being.

While it wasn't my reality, I know that this *has been* and *is* a challenge in minority cultures. Having been told to "suck it up" or "just deal with it" has been the equivalent of visiting a therapist. Too often, the coping mechanisms witnessed by young African Americans were alcohol or illicit drugs. As minority men, we are still taught that being in touch with your emotions is exhibiting feminine qualities, so we hold it *ALL* in … until we can't. And that result is a result that is a benefit to no one!

Spiritual Well-Being

Spiritual well-being involves nurturing your relationship with God and aligning your actions with your faith. Engage in regular prayer, study the Scriptures, and participate in community worship. By grounding yourself in your faith, you draw strength, guidance, and inspiration to pursue excellence in all aspects of your life. As evidenced by this work and the seven principles that are rooted in my spiritual belief, this one is most important in my opinion, regardless of its position on my list.

Excellence in Professional Life

Excellence in your professional life involves setting high standards for your work, continuously improving your skills, and delivering exceptional results. It requires a commitment to lifelong learning, effective time management, and a proactive approach to career development.

Lifelong Learning

Commit to continuous learning and skill development. Stay updated on industry trends, seek out professional development opportunities, and invest in further education. By continually enhancing your knowledge and skills, you position yourself as an expert in your field and increase your value to employers and clients. Professionals will always have a place in the market as long as they are marketing their skills and the results they deliver.

Time Management

Effective time management is crucial for achieving excellence. Prioritize your tasks, set clear goals, and allocate time for focused work. Avoid procrastination and distractions and create a structured schedule that maximizes productivity. By managing your time effectively, you can consistently deliver high-quality work and meet deadlines. This will have a profound impact on the quality of your personal life as well.

Proactive Career Development

Take charge of your career development by setting clear goals and seeking opportunities for advancement. Network strategically, seek mentorship, and be open to new challenges and responsibilities. By proactively managing your career, you can achieve professional excellence and create opportunities for growth and success.

Excellence in Community Involvement

Excellence in community involvement involves making a positive impact and contributing to the well-being of others. It requires a commitment to service, leadership, and social responsibility. By pursuing excellence in your community involvement, you can create meaningful change and inspire others to do the same.

Service

Engage in acts of service that align with your highest values and passions. Volunteer your time, skills, and resources to support causes that are important to you. By serving others with excellence, you create a positive impact and contribute to the betterment of your community. We will conclude this book by talking about the principle of Serving Others and how it can lead any minority to financial freedom.

Leadership

Take on leadership roles within your community to drive positive change. Whether through formal positions or informal influence, lead by example and inspire others to join your efforts. Effective leadership involves clear communication, empathy, and a commitment to the common good.

Social Responsibility

Embrace social responsibility by advocating for justice, equity, and sustainability. Use your influence and resources to support initiatives that address social issues and promote the well-being of all. By pursuing excellence in social responsibility, you contribute to a more just and equitable society.

Biblical Examples of Excellence

The Bible provides numerous examples of individuals who pursued excellence in various aspects of their lives. These stories offer valuable lessons and inspiration for our own pursuit of excellence.

Daniel

Daniel is a powerful example of excellence in his professional life. Despite being taken captive and brought to Babylon, Daniel distinguished himself through his exceptional wisdom, integrity, and dedication. He excelled in his studies and work, gaining favor with the king and rising to a position of high authority. Daniel 6:3 states, "Now Daniel so distinguished himself among the administrators and the satraps by his exceptional qualities that the king planned to set him over the whole kingdom." Daniel's commitment to excellence and his unwavering faith serves as a model for us to emulate.

Ruth

Ruth's story exemplifies excellence in personal relationships and community involvement. Despite facing hardship and loss, Ruth demonstrated unwavering loyalty and dedication to her mother-in-law, Naomi. Her hard work and integrity earned her the respect and admiration of the community. Ruth's commitment to excellence and her selfless service led to her becoming the great-grandmother of King David. Her story, recorded in the Book of Ruth, highlights the importance of excellence in our relationships and community contributions.

Joseph

Unsurprisingly we look at Joseph's journey from slavery to becoming a powerful leader in Egypt as a testament to excellence in adversity. Despite decades of challenges, Joseph maintained his integrity and dedication to excellence. His ability to interpret dreams and manage resources effectively led to his rise to prominence and the preservation of many lives during a famine. Joseph's story, found in Genesis 37-50, underscores the importance of excellence in all circumstances, even when faced with significant obstacles.

Bezalel

Another example is Bezalel, who was chosen by God to oversee the construction of the Tabernacle. Bezalel was endowed with exceptional skill and craftsmanship, which he used to create the intricate and beautiful furnishings for the Tabernacle. Exodus 31:2-5 describes Bezalel's abilities: "See, I have chosen Bezalel son of Uri, the son of Hur, of the tribe of Judah, and I have filled him with the Spirit of God, with wisdom, with understanding, with knowledge and with all kinds of skills—to make artistic designs for work in gold, silver and bronze, to cut and set stones, to work in wood, and to engage in all kinds of crafts."

Bezalel's excellence in his craft brought glory to God and set a high standard for others to follow. His commitment to Excel Everywhere resulted in him being featured in the greatest story that has ever been told or sold.

Modern Examples of Excellence

In modern times, individuals like Serena Williams exemplify the pursuit of excellence. Serena's dedication to her sport, rigorous training regimen, and relentless drive have made her one of the greatest tennis players of all time. Her commitment to excellence extends beyond the court, as she uses her platform to advocate for equality and empower others.

Another example is Indra Nooyi, the former CEO of PepsiCo. Known for her exceptional leadership and strategic vision, Nooyi transformed PepsiCo into a more sustainable and profitable company. Her pursuit of excellence in business leadership has earned her numerous accolades and inspired aspiring leaders around the world.

Strategies for Achieving Excellence

Achieving excellence involves a combination of mindset, habits, and practical strategies. Here are key steps to help you excel in every area of your life:

1. **Set High Standards**: Establish clear and high standards for yourself in everything you do. Strive for quality and consistency, and do not settle for mediocrity. Setting high standards motivates you to push beyond your comfort zone and achieve greater results.

2. **Be Disciplined**: Discipline is the foundation of excellence. Develop self-discipline by setting goals, creating routines, and staying committed to your objectives. Discipline enables you to stay focused and make consistent progress toward your goals.

3. **Seek Continuous Improvement**: Excellence is a journey not a destination. Continuously seek ways to improve and refine your skills. Solicit feedback from others, reflect on your performance, and implement changes that enhance your abilities. Adopt the Japanese philosophy of Kaizen, which emphasizes continuous improvement in all areas of life.

4. **Embrace Accountability**: Hold yourself accountable for your actions and outcomes. Take responsibility for your successes and failures and use them as learning experiences. Accountability fosters integrity and encourages a proactive approach to personal and professional growth.

5. **Surround Yourself with Excellence**: Surround yourself with individuals who share your commitment to excellence. Engage with mentors, peers, and role models who inspire and challenge you to be your best. Proverbs 27:17 states, "As iron sharpens iron, so one person sharpens another." Being part of a community of excellence can elevate your standards and provide valuable support.

6. **Prioritize Health and Well-being**: Your physical, mental, and emotional well-being are crucial to achieving excellence. Prioritize self-care by maintaining a healthy lifestyle, managing stress, and ensuring adequate rest. A balanced and healthy life enhances your ability to perform at your best.

7. **Focus on Purpose and Passion**: Align your efforts with your purpose and passion. When you are passionate about what you do, you are more likely to invest the time and energy required

to excel. Purpose-driven work is fulfilling and motivates you to strive for excellence.

Affluence in Action

Marcus Henderson grew up in a modest household on the south side of Chicago, raised by a single mother who worked two jobs to make ends meet. From an early age, Marcus understood that nothing would come easy, but he was determined to break the cycle of poverty that had gripped his family for generations. Excellence was always his goal, though his environment often pushed him in the opposite direction.

After excelling academically in high school, Marcus earned a scholarship to a top university, where he majored in computer science. It was there that he was first introduced to the world of tech startups and entrepreneurship. He quickly realized that ideas were only part of the equation in the tech industry—execution and excellence in every detail were what truly set successful ventures apart.

Despite graduating at the top of his class, Marcus initially struggled to land his dream job. He faced subtle but persistent barriers as a minority in an industry where very few people looked like him. Many companies doubted his leadership potential and innovation skills, but Marcus had long ago learned not to let others define his value. He remembered his mother's lessons: "You don't have to be twice as good; you just have to be undeniable."

Refusing to accept rejection as his fate, Marcus decided to take a different route. Instead of waiting for opportunities to come to him, he created his own. He launched a small tech consultancy offering data analytics services to local businesses. From the beginning, Marcus embraced a mindset of excellence. His motto was simple: "If I'm going to do it, I'm going to be the best at it."

He took no shortcuts and ensured every client received the best service he could offer. He worked late nights to stay on top of industry trends and invested in his learning. His relentless pursuit of excellence paid off. Over time, Marcus built a reputation for his technical skills, meticulous attention to detail, and commitment to delivering exceptional results.

One pivotal moment came when a major national retailer—initially skeptical of hiring a small, minority-owned firm—took a chance on Marcus's consultancy for a critical project. The stakes were high, but Marcus and his team over-delivered, providing insights that solved the retailer's problem and helped them increase their revenue by fifteen percent in a single quarter. That one project became the cornerstone of Marcus's business success. Word spread quickly, and before long, he signed contracts with Fortune 500 companies.

But Marcus didn't stop there. He wanted to ensure his success would ripple through his community. He started a mentorship program for minority students interested in tech careers, emphasizing the importance of excellence in everything they do—whether it's their academics, relationships, or future business ventures.

Today, Marcus's consultancy is a multimillion-dollar company. He remains a vocal advocate for diversity in the tech space. He often reminds his mentees that excellence isn't just about talent—it's about persistence, dedication, and the daily commitment to being better than you were the day before.

Through his journey, Marcus exemplified the principle of Excel Everywhere, demonstrating that true affluence is not just about financial wealth but about the standard of excellence you bring to every aspect of your life. He turned obstacles into opportunities, not by lowering his standards but by raising them and pushing the boundaries of what others believed possible for someone from his background.

Ideas to Action

- Identify your current level of standards for all areas of your life. (Okay, Good, Excellent)
- Identify where you are currently excelling in life.
- List the areas where excellence is not currently a reality for you and why. (No excuses allowed.)
- Who would benefit if you excelled everywhere? Call them and apologize for not doing everything in a spirit of excellence. Tell them that you will excel everywhere going forward and they will benefit as a result of your excellence.

Additional Resources

- Books: *The Pursuit of Excellence* by Terry Orlick, *Good to Great* by Jim Collins, *The Excellence Habit* by Vlad Zachary
- Organizations: Toastmasters International, American Management Association, National Society of Leadership and Success

Pursuing excellence is a continuous journey that involves setting high standards, committing to lifelong learning, and striving to perform at the highest level in all areas of life. By pursuing excellence in your personal, professional, and community endeavors, you can achieve success, make a positive impact, and inspire others to do the same.

Remember, as God's children, we are called to excellence in all we do. By dedicating ourselves fully to our tasks and striving for the highest performance standards, we honor God and fulfill our divine potential.

For bonus content visit www.TheAffluentNegroes.com/Bonus

CHAPTER 8

SERVE OTHERS

*"Use your skills, your knowledge, your instincts to serve – to go
change the world in the way that only you can."*

—Robert F. Smith

"Each of you should use whatever gift you have received to
serve others, as faithful stewards of God's grace in its various
forms." (1 Peter 4:10)

Service (noun) - The action of helping or doing work for someone;
the act of contributing to the welfare of others.

The Importance of Serving Others

Service is the selfless act of meeting the needs of others, and it lies at
the heart of biblical teaching. Serving others is not only a moral obliga-
tion but also a path to personal fulfillment, societal improvement, and
wealth creation. For minority individuals seeking to create wealth and
achieve success, a commitment to service can enhance their impact and
legacy. Serving others fosters a sense of community, creates opportunities for collaboration, and amplifies positive change.

Jesus Christ exemplified the principle of service. In Mark 10:45, He
said, "For even the Son of Man did not come to be served, but to serve,

and to give his life as a ransom for many." Jesus' life and ministry were characterized by acts of service, compassion, and sacrifice. By following His example, we can make a meaningful difference in the lives of others and in our communities.

Biblical Examples of Service

The Bible is filled with stories of individuals who demonstrated the importance of service. One such example is the Good Samaritan. (Luke 10:25-37) In this parable, Jesus tells the story of a man who was beaten and left for dead. While others passed by without helping, a Samaritan stopped, cared for the man's wounds, and ensured his recovery. This parable teaches us the value of compassion and the importance of helping those in need, regardless of their background.

Another example is Ruth, who showed extraordinary loyalty and service to her mother-in-law, Naomi. Despite facing her own hardships, Ruth committed to staying with Naomi and supporting her. Ruth's selfless service eventually led to her becoming an ancestor of King David and Jesus Christ. (Ruth 1-4) Her story highlights the rewards of serving others with a genuine heart.

In the New Testament, the Apostle Paul dedicated his life to serving others through his missionary journeys and letters. Despite facing challenges and persecution, Paul remained steadfast in his mission to spread the gospel and support the early Christian communities. His letters, such as those to the Corinthians, Ephesians, and Philippians, emphasize the importance of serving one another in love and humility.

The early Christian community also serves as a powerful example of collective service. Acts 2:44-45 describes how "All the believers were together and had everything in common. They sold property and possessions to give to anyone who had need." This sense of communal support and shared responsibility illustrates the profound impact of collective service in building a supportive and thriving community.

Modern Examples of Service

In contemporary times, individuals like Robert F. Smith, the billionaire philanthropist and CEO of Vista Equity Partners, exemplify the principle of service. Smith's generous donation to pay off the student loans of Morehouse College's graduating class of 2019 is a testament to his commitment to uplifting others. His philanthropy extends to numerous causes, including education, arts, and social justice, demonstrating how serving others can create a lasting impact.

Another modern example is Melinda Gates, co-chair of the Bill & Melinda Gates Foundation. Through her work, Gates has focused on improving global health, expanding educational opportunities, and advocating for women's rights. Her dedication to service has transformed countless lives and contributed to significant advancements in public health and education.

LeBron James, the renowned basketball player, is also a notable figure in service. Beyond his achievements on the court, James has made significant contributions to education and community development. His LeBron James Family Foundation has established the I PROMISE School in Akron, Ohio, providing resources and support to at-risk children and their families. James's commitment to service underscores the importance of giving back to the community and creating opportunities for the next generation.

The Impact of Service on Personal Growth

Serving others not only benefits those you help but also fosters personal growth and development which have both been themes permeating this entire book. Engaging in acts of service cultivates empathy, compassion, and a sense of purpose. When you serve others, you develop a deeper understanding of their struggles and challenges, which broadens your perspective and enhances your emotional intelligence.

Service also builds character and strengthens values such as humility, gratitude, and integrity. By putting the needs of others before your own, you learn to prioritize kindness and generosity which enriches your character and strengthens your moral compass. This personal growth positively impacts all areas of your life, from relationships to career success.

Furthermore, service can lead to the development of new skills and experiences. Volunteering for different causes exposes you to diverse environments and challenges, fostering adaptability and problem-solving abilities which we now know are sought after. These skills are valuable in both personal and professional contexts, enhancing your overall competence and effectiveness.

Strategies for Serving Others

Serving others involves intentional actions and a mindset of generosity. To begin, reflect on your skills, knowledge, and resources that can be used to help others. Understanding what you have to offer enables you to serve more effectively and make a greater impact. Whether it is through your professional expertise, financial resources, or personal time, identifying your strengths allows you to tailor your service efforts to areas where you can make the most significant contribution.

Next, look for opportunities to serve in your community, workplace, and beyond. Volunteer at local organizations, participate in community events, and support causes that align with your aforementioned values. Serving others can take many forms, from mentoring and tutoring to providing financial support and advocating for social justice. By actively seeking out service opportunities, you integrate the practice of giving into your daily life, making it a consistent and meaningful part of your routine.

Make service a regular part of your life by setting aside time each week or month to engage in service activities. Consistency in serving others builds lasting relationships and creates meaningful change. Regular involvement also deepens your commitment to the causes you support and allows you to witness the long-term impact of your efforts.

Approach service with a compassionate and empathetic heart, seeking to understand the needs and experiences of those you are helping. Listening and showing genuine care can make a significant difference in their lives. Empathy enhances the quality of your service, ensuring that your efforts are truly responsive to the needs of others and fostering deeper connections with those you serve.

Join forces with like-minded individuals and organizations to amplify your impact. Collaboration can lead to more comprehensive solutions and a broader reach. Building a network of service-minded individuals creates a supportive community focused on making a difference. By working together, you can pool resources, share knowledge, and coordinate efforts to tackle complex challenges more effectively.

Leverage your position, platform, and influence to advocate for positive change. Whether you are a business leader, educator, or community member, you have the power to inspire others and drive meaningful initiatives. Use your voice to raise awareness and support important causes. Public advocacy can mobilize broader support and bring attention to critical issues, amplifying the impact of your service.

Invest in the growth and development of others by providing mentorship and support. Empowering others to achieve their potential creates a ripple effect of positive change. Share your knowledge, experiences, and resources to help others succeed. Mentorship not only benefits the mentee but also enriches your own life by providing opportunities for reflection, learning, and personal connection.

Implementing Service in Various Areas

Service should be integrated into all aspects of your life, including your career, relationships, and personal development. In your professional life, look for ways to serve your colleagues, clients, and community. Offer mentorship and support to your peers, participate in corporate social responsibility initiatives, and use your expertise to benefit others.

Creating a culture of service in the workplace enhances teamwork, morale, and overall success. Companies that prioritize service and corporate responsibility often see increased employee engagement, customer loyalty, and community support.

In your personal relationships, practice service by being present, supportive, and understanding. Help family members and friends in times of need, and show appreciation for their presence in your life. Acts of kindness and generosity strengthen bonds and create a positive environment. Service within personal relationships fosters a sense of mutual support and love, enhancing the quality of your connections and contributing to a more fulfilling life.

Commit to personal growth through service. Volunteering and helping others can provide valuable learning experiences and enhance your skills. Service fosters empathy, humility, and a sense of purpose, contributing to your overall well-being and fulfillment. Engaging in service activities allows you to step outside your comfort zone, encounter diverse perspectives, and develop a more well-rounded and compassionate worldview.

Overcoming Challenges in Service

While serving others is rewarding, it can also present challenges. Balancing service commitments with personal and professional responsibilities requires careful planning and time management. Prioritize your commitments and be realistic about what you can contribute without overextending yourself. Effective time management ensures that you can fulfill your service obligations while maintaining your well-being and productivity in other areas.

Emotional challenges may arise when dealing with difficult situations or witnessing suffering. Practice self-care and seek support when needed to maintain your emotional health. Engaging in reflective practices, such as journaling or meditation, can help you process your experiences and maintain emotional resilience.

Maintaining motivation over the long term can be challenging, especially when progress seems slow, or setbacks occur. Stay connected to your purpose and remind yourself of the positive impact of your efforts. Celebrate small victories and milestones to sustain your motivation and commitment. Reflecting on the positive changes you have contributed to can reinforce your sense of purpose and drive.

The Ripple Effect of Service

Service has a ripple effect that extends beyond the immediate beneficiaries. When you serve others, you inspire those around you to do the same, creating a culture of generosity and compassion. Your actions can motivate others to get involved, amplifying the overall impact of your service. This ripple effect can lead to broader societal change, fostering a community where individuals support and uplift one another.

Moreover, your service can have lasting effects on the lives of those you help. By providing mentorship, education, or resources, you empower individuals to achieve their goals and improve their circumstances. This empowerment can lead to sustained positive outcomes, such as improved economic stability, educational attainment, and overall well-being.

The Joy of Serving Others

Serving others brings immense joy and fulfillment. The act of giving and helping others creates a sense of purpose and satisfaction that material wealth alone cannot provide. Knowing that your efforts have made a difference in someone's life brings a deep sense of happiness and contentment. This joy of service reflects the biblical principle that "It is more blessed to give than to receive." (Acts 20:35)

Furthermore, serving others fosters gratitude and appreciation for the blessings in your own life. Witnessing the challenges and resilience of others can provide perspective and inspire a greater sense of thankfulness. This gratitude enhances your overall well-being and contributes to a positive outlook on life.

Affluence in Action

Jamal grew up in the heart of Atlanta, where his family's story was one of struggle and perseverance. Raised in a small apartment in a working-class neighborhood, Jamal was no stranger to hard times. His mother worked multiple jobs to support their family after his father's untimely death when Jamal was just ten years old. Even in the face of adversity, she instilled in him a deep sense of faith, resilience, and an unwavering commitment to helping others.

From an early age, Jamal learned that success wasn't just about individual achievement. His mother always said, "You rise by lifting others." Those words stuck with him, shaping the way he saw the world. He watched his mother volunteer at the local church and organize food drives, even when she was struggling herself. Her example planted the seeds of service that would later become the foundation of Jamal's life and career.

Jamal excelled academically and earned a scholarship to attend Morehouse College, a historically black college known for producing leaders. It was at Morehouse where Jamal's commitment to service deepened. Surrounded by ambitious peers and mentors who emphasized the importance of giving back to the community, Jamal realized that success meant little if it wasn't shared.

After graduating, Jamal moved to New York City to pursue a career in finance. He aimed to build a secure financial future for himself and his family. He landed a job at a prestigious investment firm, quickly rising through the ranks. By thirty, he was earning more money than he had ever imagined. But despite his financial success, something was missing. Jamal couldn't shake the feeling that he wasn't fulfilling his true purpose.

Everything changed one evening when Jamal returned to Atlanta for a family visit. He drove through his old neighborhood and saw how much it had deteriorated since his childhood. The small businesses that once thrived were now shuttered, and families were struggling even more than before. At that moment, Jamal felt a pull to do something meaningful for his community.

Inspired by the values of service his mother had instilled in him, Jamal decided to take a bold step. He quit his high-paying job in New York and returned to Atlanta, determined to make a difference. His goal was clear: to use his financial expertise to empower black entrepreneurs and small business owners, helping them build sustainable, thriving businesses in communities like his own.

Jamal launched a financial consulting initiative focused on providing mentorship, funding, and strategic advice to minority-owned businesses in underserved areas. His mission was to close the wealth gap by giving black business owners the tools they needed to succeed.

But Jamal didn't stop at offering financial services. He knew that many of these business owners didn't just need funding—they needed mentorship, guidance, and someone to believe in them. Jamal set up a program that paired successful black professionals with aspiring entrepreneurs. Through workshops, one-on-one mentoring, and networking events, these entrepreneurs gained access to the knowledge and resources that had historically been denied to them.

One of the first businesses Jamal helped was a local barbershop owned by a man named Anthony. Anthony had been in the community for decades, cutting hair for fathers, sons, and grandsons alike. But the business had fallen on hard times, with rising rent prices and increased competition. When he met Jamal, Anthony was on the brink of closing his doors for good.

Jamal took a personal interest in Anthony's situation. He sat down with him to review his finances. He realized that with a few strategic changes—such as revising his pricing model, reducing overhead costs, and implementing targeted marketing—Anthony could turn his business around. Jamal also connected Anthony with a marketing professional from his network, who helped rebrand the shop and attract a new generation of customers.

Within a year, Anthony's barbershop was not only thriving but expanding. He opened a second location and began mentoring younger barbers in the community, paying forward the help he had received. This ripple effect was exactly what Jamal had hoped for when he started his initiative.

Another transformative moment came when Jamal provided funding for Aisha, a single mother who dreamed of opening a bakery in the same neighborhood where she grew up. Despite her undeniable talent and passion, several banks had turned her down for loans. The financial institutions saw her as a risk, but Jamal saw her potential.

Jamal's team worked closely with Aisha, helping her secure a loan, draft a business plan, and find a location. With Jamal's guidance, Aisha's bakery became an overnight success. Known for her delicious cakes and pastries, Aisha created a thriving business and employed several local residents, giving them opportunities they hadn't previously had.

Her bakery became a hub for the community, a place where people gathered to celebrate birthdays, graduations, and other milestones. Aisha's story inspired other women in the neighborhood to pursue their own entrepreneurial dreams, proving that when you invest in one person, you invest in the entire community.

Today, Jamal's efforts have helped over 100 minority-owned businesses grow and prosper, from retail stores to tech startups. His focus on service—rooted in his mother's teachings—has created a lasting impact financially, socially, and emotionally. His work is more than just a business, it's a movement that is reshaping the narrative around black entrepreneurship.

Jamal's journey exemplifies the principle of **Serve Others** in action. He has created a ripple effect of success by using his talents and resources to uplift his community. What started as a desire to help a few small businesses has turned into a mission to transform entire communities. Jamal understands that true affluence is not measured by personal wealth but by how much you contribute to the prosperity of others.

Jamal often says, "When one of us wins, we all win." His story is a testament to the power of service, the strength of community, and the impact of sharing success with those who need it most.

Ideas to Action

- Identify your strengths and resources that can be used to help others.
- Connect with a local civic organization or church to determine what service opportunities are available and which ones are a fit for you.
- If you are a believer, commit to tithing at your church. If not, set up recurring donations to a charity of your choice.
- Find a protégé to mentor and schedule regular mentorship sessions.

Additional Resources

- Books: *The Purpose Driven Life* by Rick Warren, *The Giving Way to Happiness* by Jenny Santi, *Doing Good Better* by William MacAskill

- Organizations: United Way, Habitat for Humanity, AmeriCorps

Serving others is a fundamental principle that enriches your life and creates a positive impact on those around you. By identifying your strengths and resources, seeking opportunities to serve, practicing compassion and empathy, collaborating with others, using your influence for good, and mentoring and empowering others, you can make a meaningful difference.

Remember, as God's children, we are called to serve one another in love and humility, following the example of Jesus Christ. By embracing the principle of service, you contribute to the well-being of your community, build lasting relationships, and fulfill your divine purpose.

Service is not just an action but a way of life that transforms both the giver and the receiver. It bridges gaps, builds communities, and fosters a sense of unity and purpose. As you continue your journey towards wealth creation and personal success, let service be a guiding principle that enriches your path and amplifies your impact. In doing so, you will not only achieve personal fulfillment but also leave a legacy of compassion and generosity.

For bonus content visit www.TheAffluentNegroes.com/Bonus

CHAPTER 9

THE KEY THAT DIDN'T FIT
–TITHING

"What I've learned is that you can't out-give God. You tithe. You give. God gives it back to you; He's not going to leave you hanging."

–Tyler Perry

"Honor the Lord with your wealth, with the first fruits of all your crops; then your barns will be filled to overflowing, and your vats will brim over with new wine." (Proverbs 3:9-10)

Tithing (noun) - The act of giving one-tenth of one's income or produce as an offering to the Lord, traditionally understood as a biblical principle of giving.

As we've explored the seven principles of wealth creation throughout this book—**Network Strategically, Educate Yourself, Generate Wealth Through Entrepreneurship, Reinforce Resilience, Own It All, Excel Everywhere, and Serve Others**—we've laid out a comprehensive guide to achieving financial empowerment and living a life of abundance. Each principle has its unique value, and together, they form a robust framework for overcoming obstacles and seizing opportunities.

These seven principles fit neatly into the acronym **NEGROES**, symbolizing both the path forward for minority individuals and the unity of a community rising together toward prosperity. The acronym provided a memorable structure, grounding the ideas in a holistic approach to wealth creation.

However, as we come to the end of this journey, there is one more principle we must address—one that didn't quite fit into the **NEGROES** acronym but is indispensable to everything we've discussed thus far. This principle is tithing. Think of it as the "key that didn't fit" into the acronym but one that still holds the power to unlock the door to true, lasting wealth—both material and spiritual.

Unlike the previous principles, which focus on strategies, mindsets, and actions in the external world, tithing represents a deeper, more personal form of wealth creation. It's rooted in faith, obedience, and trust in God's provision. While the other principles guide you in navigating the financial and societal landscape, tithing anchors you spiritually, ensuring that your pursuit of wealth is grounded in gratitude, stewardship, and divine purpose.

Tithing is not merely an afterthought or a minor footnote in the journey toward prosperity. It's the foundation of how we relate to the resources we receive, reminding us that we are not the ultimate owners but stewards of God's blessings. Offering a portion of our earnings serves as an acknowledgment that everything we have is a result of His grace. It is a step of faith that invites His abundance into every area of our lives— beyond just finances.

Tithing also serves as a bridge between personal wealth and community upliftment. In minority communities, churches and faith-based organizations have historically been pillars of support, education, and empowerment. They have provided spiritual guidance and resources for financial literacy, entrepreneurship, and social progress. Tithing, therefore, is a way of contributing to this collective power, fueling the growth of our communities and ensuring that our wealth is shared, circulated, and multiplied.

In this final chapter, we will explore how tithing plays an essential role in the wealth creation process, even though it didn't neatly fit into the acronym. We will uncover how this "key that didn't fit" is actually what unlocks the doors to lasting prosperity, peace of mind, and spiritual fulfillment. Tithing ties together all the principles we've covered, ensuring that your journey toward wealth is not just about financial gain but about living a life aligned with divine purpose and service to others.

The journey of **The Affluent Negroes** has always been about more than just individual success. It's about creating generational wealth, fostering community strength, and leaving a legacy of abundance that transcends financial gain. And to do this thoroughly, tithing must be part of the equation. As you consider integrating this principle into your life, remember that tithing may not fit into the acronym, but it is the key that will help you unlock the doors to everything you are working toward.

Tithing as an Act of Faith and Stewardship

Tithing is more than just a financial transaction—it's an act of faith, obedience, and stewardship. It reflects a deep trust in God as the ultimate provider and acknowledges that everything we possess comes from Him. By tithing, we affirm that we are stewards of God's resources and honor Him by returning a portion of what we have been given.

For minority individuals and communities seeking to create wealth, tithing is a personal act of faith and a collective practice that can fuel broader community development. Historically, churches and faith communities have significantly supported minority wealth creation by fostering unity, providing financial resources, and offering educational opportunities.

In the context of wealth creation, tithing reminds us that financial success is not solely due to our efforts but is also a blessing from God. Tithing helps us keep a balanced perspective, ensuring that we don't become consumed by material wealth but remain grounded in our spiritual responsibilities. Additionally, it connects us to the well-being of others, contributing to the collective advancement of minority communities.

Building Generational Wealth Through Giving

One of the most potent aspects of tithing in minority wealth creation is its ability to create generational wealth. By contributing to community institutions and supporting educational programs, minority individuals who tithe are enriching their lives and creating opportunities for future generations. For example, many historically Black colleges and universities (HBCUs) have been sustained through the financial contributions of church congregations and faithful tithers who believed in the power of education to transform lives and elevate communities.

The Connection Between Tithing and Wealth Creation

Tithing plays a significant role in wealth creation, particularly in minority communities, but not necessarily in the way the world might define it. While tithing does not guarantee instant financial returns or material riches, it aligns us with divine principles of giving, stewardship, and generosity that lay the foundation for sustainable prosperity.

1. **Tithing and Generosity:** Generosity is crucial in wealth creation, particularly for minority individuals who understand the power of collective upliftment. When we tithe, we cultivate a spirit of generosity, which can profoundly affect our financial lives. As Luke 6:38 says, "Give, and it will be given to you. A good measure, pressed down, shaken together, and running over, will be poured into your lap. For with the measure you use, it will be measured to you." Tithing teaches us to live with

an open hand, trusting that God will replenish what we give with even greater abundance.

2. **Tithing and Discipline:** One key to creating wealth is discipline, and tithing cultivates financial discipline. By committing to give a tenth of our income, we develop a habit of budgeting, planning, and prioritizing our finances. This practice extends beyond the tithe, fostering wise financial management that is essential for wealth creation. For many minority individuals, developing this kind of financial discipline has been a path to stability and long-term wealth.

3. **Tithing and Gratitude:** Wealth creation is not just about accumulating money; it's also about maintaining a mindset of gratitude. Tithing is an expression of thankfulness to God for His blessings. This attitude of gratitude fosters contentment and helps us avoid the pitfalls of greed and materialism, which can derail our financial journey. Gratitude also strengthens communal bonds, as tithing connects us with the collective efforts of lifting others within our community. By fostering a sense of gratitude, tithing helps us appreciate our financial situation and find contentment—regardless of the amount of wealth we have accumulated.

4. **Tithing and Faith:** Building wealth often involves taking risks and stepping out in faith, whether through entrepreneurship, investments, or career advancements. Tithing strengthens our faith by reminding us that God is our ultimate provider. When we tithe, we express trust that God will meet our needs, even as we give away a portion of what we have. This faith in God's provision empowers us to pursue opportunities for wealth creation with confidence and peace.

5. **Tithing and Community:** Tithing is not only about personal financial growth, it also supports the broader community. In

biblical times, tithes were used to support the priests, the temple, and those in need. Today, our tithes contribute to the functioning of our churches and the well-being of those less fortunate. In many minority communities, churches are central hubs for community support, providing everything from financial literacy workshops to business grants and educational scholarships. By tithing, we participate in the cycle of blessing, where our generosity enables others to thrive, and in turn, we are blessed.

Minority Examples of Generosity Leading to Wealth and Success

Many minority figures exemplify the principle that generosity, whether through tithing or philanthropy, can lead to personal success and communal upliftment.

1. **Madam C.J. Walker:** As the first self-made African American woman millionaire, Madam C.J. Walker built a beauty empire during the early 20th century. Her success was not just about creating wealth for herself, she was known for her generous giving. Walker was a prominent supporter of Black colleges, the YMCA, and many other philanthropic causes that empowered African American communities. Walker's success was deeply intertwined with her commitment to giving back, demonstrating how generosity can pave the way for personal and collective wealth creation.

2. **Robert F. Smith:** As the wealthiest Black man in America, Robert F. Smith has made headlines for his extraordinary generosity. In 2019, Smith famously announced during a commencement address at Morehouse College that he would pay off the student loans for the entire graduating class. This contribution changed the financial future of hundreds of young Black men. Smith's philanthropic work extends beyond this, with his foundation

focusing on closing the opportunity gap for marginalized communities. His example highlights how wealth creation and generosity go hand in hand, especially within minority communities where such acts of giving can have generational impacts.

3. **Daymond John:** Known for his role on *Shark Tank* and as the founder of FUBU, Daymond John is not only a successful entrepreneur but also a dedicated philanthropist. John gives back to communities by supporting entrepreneurial education, particularly for young people of color. He has emphasized the importance of financial literacy and generosity in creating sustainable wealth. John's approach to philanthropy mirrors the principles of tithing, showing that success is multiplied when we invest in others.

4. **LeBron James:** As one of the most successful athletes of all time, LeBron James has used his wealth to give back to the community. Through his LeBron James Family Foundation, he has opened the I PROMISE School in Akron, Ohio, providing education, meals, and services to at-risk children. James's commitment to community upliftment reflects the principle of tithing—giving back a portion of what you have received to benefit others, ensuring that success becomes a collective endeavor.

5. **Katherine Johnson:** While not as financially wealthy as some of the other figures mentioned, Katherine Johnson's legacy of generosity can be seen in her commitment to education and mentorship. Johnson, the famed mathematician who contributed to NASA's space missions, used her platform to advocate for STEM education, particularly for young African American girls. Her willingness to invest in others through her time, knowledge, and mentorship created a ripple effect of success, proving that tithing one's resources isn't always monetary—it can be intellectual and social capital.

Breaking the Scarcity Mentality in Minority Communities

For many minority individuals, historical and systemic barriers have fostered a scarcity mentality—the belief that there is never enough to go around. This mindset can lead to fear, hoarding, and an inability to give freely. Tithing helps to break this cycle by shifting our focus from scarcity to abundance. It challenges us to trust in God's provision and believe He will meet our needs as we honor Him with our finances.

Minority communities that embrace collective giving, whether through tithing or community-driven philanthropy, often see a significant transformation. Churches, social organizations, and community groups have long been the backbone of support for marginalized communities, and tithing is the spiritual and financial fuel that allows these institutions to thrive. This collective giving creates opportunities for education, housing, business ownership, and community advancement.

How Tithing Leads to Financial Freedom

Although it may seem counterintuitive, tithing can lead to financial freedom. By giving away a portion of our income, we detach ourselves from the love of money and the fear of scarcity. This detachment allows us to experience financial peace, knowing that our security is not found in material wealth but in God's provision.

Tithing also helps us develop healthy financial habits. It encourages us to budget, prioritize our spending, and live within our means. When practiced consistently, these habits lead to financial freedom by reducing debt, increasing savings, and promoting wise investments. For minority individuals, this economic freedom often means breaking generational cycles of poverty and creating new paths toward prosperity and empowerment.

Actionable Steps to Begin Tithing

1. **Start Where You Are:** If tithing ten percent feels overwhelming, begin with a smaller percentage and increase it over time. The important thing is to cultivate a heart of generosity and a willingness to give.

2. **Budget for Your Tithe:** Incorporate tithing into your budget like any other financial commitment. Treat it as a priority, not an afterthought.

3. **Be Consistent:** Tithing is most effective when it becomes a regular practice. Set a weekly, biweekly, or monthly schedule and stick to it.

4. **Give Cheerfully:** As you give, do so with a joyful heart, knowing that your tithe is an act of worship and trust in God's provision.

5. **Test God's Faithfulness:** Take God at His word in Malachi 3:10 and test His promise. As you tithe, expect God to meet your needs and bless you in ways that may extend beyond finances.

Tithing is a powerful principle that aligns with the wealth creation journey, particularly for minority individuals seeking to break cycles of scarcity and create generational wealth. It cultivates generosity, faith, discipline, and stewardship—critical financial success and spiritual growth components. By honoring God with our finances and embracing the spirit of collective upliftment, we position ourselves and our communities for lasting success and empowerment.

The examples of biblical and modern-day minority figures show that giving generously—whether through tithing or philanthropy—has profound personal and financial benefits. The act of giving unlocks new possibilities for growth, peace, and wealth, ensuring that prosperity becomes a shared blessing for generations to come.

EMBRACING THE JOURNEY TO WEALTH CREATION

As we conclude *The Affluent Negroes: 7 Principles for Minority Wealth Creation*, it is essential to reflect on the journey we have undertaken together. This book has been designed to empower you with practical strategies and timeless principles to achieve financial prosperity and personal fulfillment. By embracing the seven principles encapsulated in the acronym NEGROES—Network Strategically, Educate Yourself, Generate Wealth Through Entrepreneurship, Reinforce Resilience, Own It All, Excel Everywhere, and Serve Others—you are equipped to overcome obstacles, seize opportunities, and create a legacy of abundance.

Network Strategically

Networking is a cornerstone of success. By cultivating meaningful relationships and leveraging your connections, you can access resources, gain insights, and open doors that would otherwise remain closed. Remember the importance of authenticity, reciprocity, and continuous engagement in building a robust network.

Educate Yourself

Education is a lifelong journey that empowers you to make informed decisions and adapt to changing circumstances. Commit to continuous learning and self-improvement, and seek knowledge from diverse sources. An educated mind is a powerful tool for creating wealth and achieving your goals.

Generate Wealth Through Entrepreneurship

Entrepreneurship is a powerful vehicle for wealth creation. By embracing an entrepreneurial mindset, taking calculated risks, and developing innovative solutions, you can create value and generate wealth. Remember the importance of strategic planning, resilience, and continuous improvement in your entrepreneurial journey.

Reinforce Resilience

Resilience is the ability to persevere and adapt in the face of adversity. Cultivate a resilient mindset by developing a strong sense of purpose, embracing a positive outlook, and seeking support from others. Resilience enables you to navigate setbacks and continue moving forward toward your goals.

Own It All

Taking ownership of your life and circumstances is crucial for achieving financial independence. Conduct a thorough financial assessment, set clear goals, and develop a comprehensive plan to achieve them. Embrace accountability, self-discipline, and continuous improvement as you take control of your financial future.

Excel Everywhere

Excellence is a habit that sets you apart and opens doors to new opportunities. Strive for high standards in everything you do, embrace a growth mindset, and seek continuous improvement. Excellence is not about perfection but about giving your best effort and consistently delivering high-quality results.

Serve Others

Service is the selfless act of meeting the needs of others. By serving others with compassion and empathy, you create a positive impact and foster a sense of community. Service enriches your life, builds lasting relationships, and amplifies your legacy.

Final Reflections

As you continue your journey to wealth creation, remember that these principles are interconnected and mutually reinforcing. Each principle builds on the others, creating a comprehensive approach to achieving financial prosperity and personal fulfillment. Embrace the journey with determination, resilience, and a commitment to excellence.

Draw strength from your faith, your community, and your unique gifts and talents. Recognize that you have the power to shape your future and create a legacy of abundance for yourself and future generations.

Thank you for taking this journey with me. I hope that *The Affluent Negroes: 7 Principles for Minority Wealth Creation* has inspired and empowered you to pursue your dreams and achieve your goals. Remember, wealth creation is not just about accumulating material wealth but about living a life of purpose, fulfillment, and positive impact. Embrace these principles, stay committed to your vision, and let your journey to wealth creation be a testament to the power of faith, resilience, and service.

It has been said, "A good book can change lives."

I pray this is a good book.

CONNECT AND CONTACT

World Renowned Coaching & Consulting, LLC
ClientCare@WorldRenownedCoaching.com
786.897.4832

Scan the QR code for social media links
and FREE bonus content.

ACKNOWLEDGMENTS

No journey is ever completed alone, especially one as profound as writing this book. This work is a testament to the support, guidance, and love of the many people who have shaped my path and continue to inspire me daily.

First and foremost, my deepest thanks go to Wife. You are my anchor and my most significant source of strength. Your unwavering love, patience, and belief in me have been the foundation upon which I've built this book and my entire life. Your partnership makes everything I do possible, and for that, I am eternally grateful.

To my son, Neal Oates III (Trey), your personality, curiosity, and presence constantly remind me of the legacy I hope to leave. You inspire me to be the best version of myself every day, and I hope this work guides you as you pursue your dreams and passions. I'm proud to be your father, and I know your future is filled with greatness.

To my brothers, Steven and Curtis, you have been my lifelong companions, my first friends, and my constant sources of wisdom and encouragement. Thank you for constantly pushing me to be my best, keeping me grounded, and reminding me of the power of perseverance.

To my mother, Patricia, your love and guidance have shaped the man I am today. You taught me the values of faith, hard work, and integrity. I can never thank you enough. Your sacrifices and belief in my dreams have carried me through the most challenging times.

To my father, "Big Neal," who passed away in 2008, your example of hard work, commitment, and friendship continues to guide me daily. You never met a stranger, and your spirit of kindness and generosity is missed more than words can express. Your legacy lives on in everything I do, and I strive to carry the values you instilled in me—integrity, perseverance, and the importance of treating everyone like family. Thank you for being my first role model and for shaping the man I've become.

I am deeply grateful to my "Dirty Dozen" advisors, a group of extraordinary individuals whose wisdom and counsel have been invaluable in my personal and professional growth. You challenge me, support me, and never let me settle for anything less than excellence. You have been the sounding board for my dreams and the voice of reason when I needed it most.

To the dedicated agents at World Renowned Real Estate, thank you for believing in our shared vision of excellence and for working tirelessly to uphold the standard we have set. Your hard work, professionalism, and passion inspire me daily, and I am honored to lead such a remarkable team.

To my coaches and mentors, past and present, I owe a great deal of my success to your guidance. You have shaped not only my career but my character. Your willingness to invest your time and wisdom in me is something I will never take for granted, and I carry your lessons with me in all that I do.

To my coaching clients who trust me with your futures, you are why I do what I do. Thank you for allowing me to walk alongside you in your journeys. Your dedication, resilience, and courage inspire me, and I am privileged to participate in your success stories. Together, we are creating a legacy of wealth, service, and excellence.

To my church family, your love, support, and prayers have been a constant source of strength and encouragement. You remind me daily of the importance of faith, community, and service. I am blessed to walk this journey of faith with each of you.

To my G.S.O. Boiz and the Giggle Golf Gang, thank you for the laughter, the camaraderie, and the much needed breaks from the daily grind. Whether on the green or off, your friendship keeps me balanced and brings me joy. You prove that excellence can be pursued with a healthy dose of humor and fun.

Lastly, I want to thank God for guiding my steps and for every blessing, challenge, and opportunity. This book reflects His grace and the many people He has placed in my life to help me along the way.

This work is as much yours as it is mine, and I am grateful beyond words. Thank you all for being part of my journey.

ABOUT THE AUTHOR

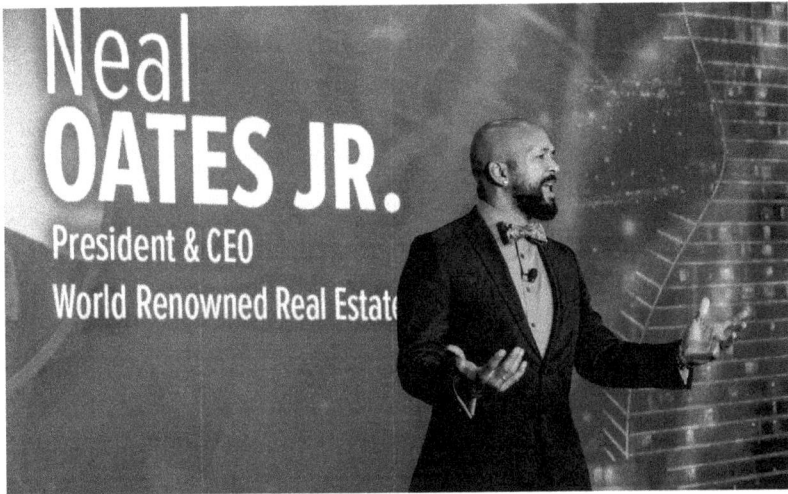

Neal Oates, Jr. is a dynamic entrepreneur, executive coach, and thought leader dedicated to empowering minority business owners and entrepreneurs to create wealth and succeed in service-based industries. As the founder and CEO of World Renowned Coaching & Consulting, Neal has made it his mission to help others unlock their full potential, scale their businesses, and serve affluent clientele with excellence. Through his coaching programs, Neal specializes in guiding minority-owned companies toward sustainable growth while fostering confidence, leadership, and a mindset for success.

Born in Florala, Alabama, Neal's journey to success was marked by resilience, faith, and a commitment to personal growth. After relocating to

South Florida at the age of twenty-three, Neal initially found success in the real estate industry. Still, his passion for teaching, mentoring, and helping others ultimately led him to expand his focus to coaching and consulting. Recognizing that many minority business owners struggled to break into higher-end markets and build generational wealth, Neal saw an opportunity to create a coaching program specifically designed to address these challenges.

In 2022, he founded World Renowned Coaching & Consulting, which has since grown into a thriving business with a reputation for transforming service-based companies into profitable, sustainable ventures. Neal's coaching focuses on helping business owners increase revenue, improve efficiency, and deliver world-class service to their clientele. His work is grounded in the belief that success in the affluent market is not only possible but achievable for minority entrepreneurs with the right strategies and mindset.

Through personalized executive coaching, group coaching programs, and workshops, Neal has helped his clients double their revenue while reducing their workload, teaching them how to attract high-value clients and operate with greater efficiency. His unique approach emphasizes the importance of believing in oneself, delivering excellence, and building a business that reflects both personal values and professional aspirations. Neal's coaching style is results-driven, and he has helped countless entrepreneurs overcome limiting beliefs, expand their influence, and position their businesses for long-term success.

Neal's coaching philosophy is built on four foundational pillars: **Excellence, Service, Leadership, and Growth**—principles he applies not only in business but also in life. He aims to show minority entrepreneurs that they can thrive in spaces traditionally dominated by others and that their success can be a catalyst for uplifting their communities.

One of Neal's most fulfilling roles is mentoring and guiding individuals who may have been overlooked or underestimated in their respective fields.

Having experienced "imposter syndrome" early in his career, Neal understands the doubts and challenges that many business owners face. His coaching is designed not only to provide practical business strategies but also to instill a deep sense of self-worth and confidence in his clients, empowering them to reach levels of success they may not have thought possible.

In addition to his coaching and consulting work, Neal is a sought-after speaker and trainer, frequently presenting at industry conferences and events. His ability to connect with audiences and share actionable insights has earned him recognition as a leader in coaching and minority business development spaces.

Though his coaching business has seen rapid growth, Neal's commitment to giving back remains a central part of his life. Through his work, he strives to make an impact beyond individual success stories—his vision is to create generational change by empowering business owners to build legacies of wealth and service. His faith is a driving force in his work, and he believes strongly in the principle of tithing and giving back both financially and through mentorship to the communities and individuals who need it most.

Outside of his business endeavors, Neal enjoys spending quality time with his wife Joanna and their son, Neal Oates, III. He credits his family and his faith as the foundation of his success, and they continue to inspire his dedication to helping others achieve greatness.

Neal Oates, Jr. has built a career by showing others what is possible—whether in business, personal growth, or community impact. His message to everyone he encounters is simple: **"Don't be average. Be world-renowned."** Through his coaching, consulting, and leadership, Neal is helping a new generation of minority business owners transform their futures and create a legacy of excellence.

Visit
www.TheAffluentNegroes.com
to schedule a complimentary
Discovery Call Today!

I love you. God loves you.
And there's nothing you can do about it!

www.ingramcontent.com/pod-product-compliance
Lightning Source LLC
Chambersburg PA
CBHW071426210326
41597CB00020B/3676